A GLIMPSE OF SOPLEY

by Sam Morris

The photograph on the cover is of a painting produced in 1816 by C. Etheridge, Ringwood.
The painting was loaned by Rachel Mooring-Aldridge.

First published in 1989 by Sam Morris, No. 17, Sopley,
near Christchurch, Dorset, BH23 7AX.

Typeset and printed by Lifespan Printing Collective,
Townhead, Dunford Bridge, Sheffield   S30 6TG.

© Sam Morris 1989

ISBN   951451 6 0 X   A Glimpse of Sopley. (pbk)

All rights reserved. No part of this publication may be transmitted or reproduced, stored in a retrieval system, or translated into any language, in any form or by any means, electronic or mechanical, including photocopying, without the prior consent of the author and publisher.

Contents

Foreword	5
Acknowledgements	6
Bibliography	7
Early Days	8
Afene	12
Worship	15
Domesday and Beyond	30
The Miller's Tale	35
The Squire's Tale	41
The Common Lands of Sopley	53
Wills	59
Poverty	67
Population	70
Commutation of Tithes	72
Roads and Traffic	79
Flight Over the Avon	85
The Work of the Parish Council	87
Education	90
Some Sopley Worthies	94
The War to End All War	105
Sopley Serves Again	108
Sopley Miscellany	115
Perambulation	119
Century of Memories	127
Appendix 1. Land Tax 1816	142
Appendix 2. Water	143

Foreword

Sopley lies astride the B3347 road between Ringwood and Christchurch, very roughly half way between the two. It remains in Hampshire by the skin of its teeth, although it shares a Dorset address with Christchurch, some three miles away. Wooed by two counties! The New Forest marches close to its eastern flank, and within living memory the Forest ponies could be seen wandering in its midst.

When I first thought of compiling a book about Sopley, my ambition was to explore the story of the whole parish. As research developed it soon became clear to me that the project would be too wide for one publication if I wanted to maintain the kind of coverage I had in mind.

I therefore decided to concentrate my attention on the village rather than the parish of Sopley, although I realised that there were certain topics which could not be dealt with solely within the isolation of the village boundaries. The chapters which follow are a result of that decision.

The book is called *A Glimpse of Sopley* advisedly, for a glimpse means an incomplete view, as this inevitably must be. It does not pretend to be a history in the more academic sense of the word. It is rather an attempt to capture and record a few impressions of a rich historical territory which I have invaded with wonderment and, I hope, humility.

Sopley 1988. *Sam Morris.*

Acknowledgements

My very grateful thanks are due to:
Miss R.C. Dunhill, County Archivist, Hampshire Record Office, and her staff; Hugh Jacques, County Archivist, and his staff at Dorchester Record Office; Alison Carter, Curator Red House Museum, Christchurch, and her staff; Michael Edgington and his staff at the Lansdowne Reference Library, Bournemouth; Bernard Green (Group Librarian) and Mrs J. Daniel, Head Librarian at Christchurch Library; the Editor, Evening Echo, Bournemouth; the General Manager, Advertiser Group, Poole; Malcolm Bale, Lieutenant Colonel, Salvation Army; the Household Cavalry Regt; the Trustees of the Kemp-Welch estate; the Vicar and Churchwardens, St Michael and All Angels Church, Sopley; the Chairman of the Sopley Commoners; the Chairman and Secretary of the Sopley Parish Council; local historian Arthur Lloyd for putting me right on certain details of ancient history, for giving me access to his own research, and for making available translations of various charters of the *Christchurch Cartulary*, made some twenty years ago by Austin Willson.

I was fortunate enough to be able to study at length at the Red House Museum the Sopley Tithe Rent Charge Apportionment Map and its accompanying register (Benjamin Love, 1851); also to read the late Dr Reginald Little's painstaking and detailed typescript of the history of Sopley Parish. Although much of what I have assembled concerns different areas of study, the sheer industry and acumen which stand out from his pages have encouraged me to persevere when my energy has flagged.

Response from the village and "neighbouring shores" has been overwhelming. Here are names of those who have exercised their memories and/or have loaned material, much of which has had to be left out through sheer pressure of space: Phyllis Bailey (née Harrison), Montie Bates, Betty Bromfield, Jeremy Bromfield, Margaret Burrett, Margaret Dacombe, May Edwards (née Harrison), Tom Entwhistle, Pam Farwell, William Farwell, Francis L.J. and Iris Freeman, John Green, Geoffrey Grindle, Mary Hallett (née Perry), Bob and Beryl Harrison, Charles and Violet Harrison, Doris Harrison, Reg Harrison, Wing-Commander F.J. Higham OBE, DFC, Frances Humphrey, Dorothy Lambert, Ruth Lavender, David Lay, Roy Mitchell, Rachel Mooring-Aldridge, May Mould (née Berryman), David Miles, David Ott, Tony Pascoe, Pat Philip, Helen Pine, Miles Rich, Mary Russell, Olive Samuel, Rev. Alan Sessford, Brian Sims, Derek, Don and Winnie Slade, Jim Tuck, Kate White, Phyllis Whittle.

I have to thank Harry Mitchell for suggesting the title of the book; John Rowley-Morris for numerous painstaking camera sessions; Bob Harrison for guiding me round the village in the fullest sense of the words.

I am much indebted to Basil White for help with maps and buildings and for permission to reproduce a few of his splendid drawings.

Finally I am ever-mindful of the ceaseless encouragement of my wife Jane, and her toleration of my frequent and often lengthy periods of isolation.

1989 S.M.

Bibliography

Victoria County History of Hampshire.
Half a Century of Sport in Hampshire. F.G. Aflado ed.
The Parish Church of St Michael and All Angels. Dacombe & Rowe.
Kelly's Directory for Hampshire.
Directory of Hampshire 1857.
History of Hampshire. William White.
New Forest Documents. A.D. 1244-1344. D.J. Stagg.
The Hampshire Avon. B. Vesey Fitzgerald.
Hampshire Parish Register (Marriages) Vol. 7.
Sopley & Vale of Avon Magazine.
Sopley, Burton, Vale of Avon Magazine.
Bournemouth & Avon Parish Magazine.
The Hampshire Magazine.
History of Hampshire. T.W. Shore.
The New Forest, Its History & Scenery. J. Wise.
Christchurch Miscellany. H. Druitt.
The Common Lands of Hampshire. L.E. Tavener.
The Thirteenth Century. F.M. Powicke.
The Turnpike Road System in England. 1663-1840. W. Albert.
The Parish Chest. W.E. Tate.
Warner's Companion 1789.
The Age of the Chartists. 1832-54. Hammond & Hammond.
Oxford Dictionary of the Christian Church. F.L. Cross ed.
General History of Hampshire. Woodward.
Rural Encyclopaedia. Rev. J.M. Wilson ed.
The Village Labourer. Hammond & Hammond.
The Anglo-Saxon Chronicle. Trans. by Benjamin Thorpe 1861.
Lay Subsidy Rolls 1586. H.R. Davey.
Proceedings of Hampshire Field Club Vol. 8.
Anglo-Saxon England. F.M. Stenton.
Minsters and Parish Churches. John Blair ed.

Early Days

The earliest inhabitants of Hampshire were the River Drift People from the Early Stone or Palaeolithic Age and some of their relics have been found in the beds of gravel along the course of the River Avon, near Christchurch and Fordingbridge. In these very early times, the valleys through which Hampshire waters now flow were in the process of being made. Since then the waters have dug deeper, while wind, rain and floods have smoothed down the sides of the valleys. The general surface of the land seems then to have been higher than it is now and the coastline further out.

Probably the Neolithic (New Stone Age) people, who provided the earliest human remains in the county, arrived soon after Britain emerged from the Glacial Drift period. They were a race with long and comparatively narrow skulls, and the long barrows which abound were their burial places. The unusually large size of these barrows has prompted the development of a whole tapestry of folk-lore concerning the exploits and last resting places of giants. Bevois and Ascupart, former antagonists who became companions in arms, are prominent in the story, as is Onion, the Giant of Silchester, and the Danish giant Colbrand, reputedly slain in single combat at Winchester by Guy of Warwick.

Round barrows are later, the sepulchres of the Bronze Age people, a race with broad and comparatively round skulls. Tin was a very important ingredient in the manufacture of bronze. Hampshire does not appear to have produced tin, but trade in tin, in the 4th century B.C., is the earliest example of trade within its ports. The development of bronze tools facilitated the clearance of land. There is considerable evidence of cremation in round barrows, and in or near the New Forest, urns and implements of stone and bronze have been found in barrows at Minstead, Burley, Buttsash, Bratley Plain, and Sopley. Bronze tools and weapons have been found at Hinton, near Christchurch.

The early cycle of 'mineral' ages was completed with the arrival of the Iron Age and the great Celtic immigration, pushing their predecessors further inland or absorbing them. The earliest Iberic peoples had been largely nomadic in their habits, while these later Celts were a typical branch of the great Aryan race who tilled the land and were more stationary in consequence. The Belgae blended into one of the most powerful of pre-Roman tribes; specific reminders of their presence in the Sopley area are gold coins. A brass coin of Faustina the Elder was found at Mudeford in 1809 and three more Roman coins have been discovered, one in Sopley meadows, one in Derritt Lane, and one on the Avon Tyrell estate in 1940; but further details of these remain obscure.

9: Early Days

Many and various are the problems encountered when trying to shed light on the local story of the Germanic invasions and the prelude to them. Two possibilities posed by the 19th century historian Woodward have provoked much debate and many counter suggestions. His theory concerning the mound on which Sopley's St Michael's Church stands was that it was the monument of some ancient battle; perhaps between Vespasian's Romans and the Belgae, perhaps between Romanised Britons and their Teutonic invaders. He asks whether Sopley may not have been the scene of a battle between Emrys and Cerdic. Suppose Cerdic to have landed at Calshot and advanced by Lymington, he would one thinks try the ford just above Sopley. If Emrys, falling back from the coast, took advantage of the entrenchment on St Catherine's Hill to the west, occupied the ford, and there posted a body of men to oppose the invaders' further progress westward, Cerdic would be forced to ascend the river to Charford (Cerdic's Ford) where we may fix his passage over the Avon.

A few extracts from the Anglo-Saxon Chronicle shed a little local light on the shadowy movements of those times:

> **495 AD:** *"In this year came two leaders to Britain, Cerdic and Cynric his son, with five ships, at the place which is called Cerdices Ora (Calshot) and on the same day they fought against the Welsh."*
>
> **508 AD:** *"In this year Cerdic and Cynric slew a British king, whose name was Natanleod, and 5000 men with him; after that the land was named Natanlea as far as Cerdices ford (Charford)."*
>
> **519 AD:** *"In this year Cerdic and Cynric assumed the kingdom of the West Saxons; and in the same year they fought against the Britons where it is now called Cerdicsford, and since, the royal offspring of the West Saxons has reigned from that day."*
>
> **527 AD:** *"In this year Cerdic and Cynric fought against the Britons at a place which is called Cerdices Leag (Charford Parish woodland)."*
>
> **530 AD:** *"In this year Cerdic and Cynric took the island of Wight and slew many men at Wihtgarasburgh (Carisbrooke)."*
>
> **534 AD:** *"In this year Cerdic, the first king of the West Saxons, died and Cynric his son succeeded to the kingdom and reigned on for 26 (27) winters."*

10: Early Days

One of the beauties of the Anglo-Saxon Chronicle is that the chronicler is not backward in showing the breadth of his vision. For the year 538 AD we find the following entry:

> *"In this year the sun was eclipsed, fourteen days before the Kalends of March (February 16th) from early morning until 9.00 a.m."*

The region which witnessed conflicts over rights of settlement for several centuries before the Norman invasion of 1066, has been described as land with three types of surface. There are barren, flat-topped plateaus and sandy plains; richer well-drained clays and loams where older geological series are exposed; and broad areas of low-lying, ill-drained marshlands. The land contained some of the poorest soils in southern England. William Cobbett, writing of its condition as late as the 19th century, says of the New Forest (the central part of it):

> *"There it is, an acre of it not having upon the average, so much of productive capacity on it as one single square rod, taking the average for Worcestershire."*

It is interesting to note that the same Anglo-Saxon Chronicle of 893 AD describes the Sussex weald as being connected by continuous woodland with the forest district of south-western Hampshire. And in the 11th century, part, if not the whole of the New Forest, still bore the name Andred. The chronicler, Florence of Worcester, writes later that William II died in the New Forest which is called *Ytene*. This name represents the genitive plural of a nominative *Yte*, which is the later West Saxon form of the Venerable Bede's *Jutae*. This seems to bolster other, perhaps less conclusive evidence, that the early Germanic invaders of the lands around Sopley were of Jutish origin.

The name Sopley can be read as the *glade of Soppa*. The man called Soppa has left nothing in the coffers of history beyond the modern place name which tells us that he settled in this countryside in Saxon times.

Older maps of the Sopley area mark the site of a battle between Saxons and Danes just north of Derritt Lane and east of Merryfield Copse. Persistent local tradition has seized upon local names as time-honoured evidence of the outcome of this confrontation; interpretations are quite contradictory. *Derritt* has been said by some to derive from *Danes' Rout*. *Harpway*, the lane leading directly from Sopley farm to the Lamb Inn, indicates, others have argued, the scene of victorious Danish carousals and harp playing. Real evidence of a fight in the locality seems as credible as the belief that the caprifoliacious shrub, *Sambucus ebulus*, owes its redness and its common name, Daneswort, to the

11: Early Days

spilled blood of Danish warriors. One botanical dictionary pronounces its flower to be white! Since about 1950 Ordnance Survey maps no longer show this battle site.

An aerial view of modern Sopley.
Photograph loaned by Montie Bates.

Afene

From the days when the haze of early history is as haunting as the mist in the Avon Valley at dawn on a summer's day, the River Avon has been an outstanding feature of the countryside which was to become Sopley Parish, so much so that the village might well have been called Sopley upon Avon.

Ghosts abound in the countryside where the waters of the Avon (*Afene* in Anglo-Saxon times), flow on their course to Christchurch Bay. Lest it become intoxicated with the richness of the historical fare afforded to it as it journeys, many springs of fresh water supply it and its meadows with a refreshing dilution as it nears the end of its journey. Many secrets must remain fast in its keep. Its part in the story of Hampshire and neighbouring counties when Stonehenge was being constructed, when the disciplined legions of Rome were afoot, when the strategy of Cerdic engaged the attention of his foes, when a treacherous, or wayward, regicide of knightly rank galloped westwards from the New Forest, is referred to elsewhere.

The course of the Avon is sixty-seven miles long with a catchment basin of 666 square miles. It drains chalk country and its waters are very clear. It does not rise and fall with suddenness; when rainfall is low it remains reasonably full when mightier rivers are reduced to little more than a trickle.

At the beginning of the nineteenth century, Royalty fishing in the Avon yielded 1600 salmon, but by 1860 this abundance had almost disappeared. Illegal netting across the run at Mudeford and dams at Knapp Mill and Winkton, prevented fish in significant numbers from swimming up the river to their spawning grounds in the higher reaches. In 1862 fixed nets across the mouth of the river and in the harbour were declared illegal and at the same time fish passes were constructed in the weirs at Knapp and at Winkton. Within two years there were more breeding fish in the river than had been noted for as long time.

A new fishing difficulty now arose owing to a complicated system of irrigation, water being taken from the main stream by large cuttings divided into smaller ones. These were again sub-divided into smaller ones until they became barely a foot in width. From these narrow channels the fish could escape in their descent to the sea. The difficulty was met to a considerable extent by a system of rewards and payments to 'drowners' or watermen who attended to irrigation. In this way many desperate wanderers were returned to the main stream. In April 1864, at Clapcote Hole, Sopley, a salmon was caught weighing upwards of 38lb, 40 inches long and 26 inches round.

The river has long been famous for its salmon and also for its eels. Anyone contemplating the yearly rental of eels payable to the lord of the manor by the miller and recorded in *Domesday*, might be forgiven for wondering how

13: Afene

the river managed to provide such a slithery annual harvest. Forgiven that is until an inspection of the traps reveals the prodigious numbers yielded up in one night of high water in our own time. Writing in 1839 John Wise referred to the peculiarity of the Avon eel, locally called the 'sniggle' (*Anguilla mediorostris*) which differs from the common eel (*acutirostris*) in its slender and elongated under-jaw and its habit of roving and feeding by day. *Collins Dictionary*'s definition for *sniggle* is threefold:

> *1. To fish for eels by dangling or thrusting a baited hook into cavities.*
> *2. To catch eels by sniggling.*
> *3. The baited hook used for sniggling eels.*

There is part of Dowle Mead, on the eastern bank of the main river at Sopley which is called Snig Half.

Roughly parallel to the Sopley mill-race as it flows past Sopley, is the 'Woolpack' stream, often known quite simply as the brook or Sopley Brook. It rises near Burley and flows into the Avon a short distance below the mill. Sea trout make their way upstream to their spawning grounds in the higher waters so that together with the eels, which are certainly partly nocturnal in their habits, an interesting and mercifully silent two-way traffic is proceeding at night while most of the inhabitants of Sopley are sleeping between the two watery thoroughfares.

It was during the reign of Charles II that Sopley's proximity to the River Avon and the New Forest might have led to a spectacular involvement in trading and defence schemes of great national importance. The Earl of Clarendon commissioned a celebrated London hydrographer named Captain Yarranton to explore and report upon the possibilities of rendering the River Avon navigable as far as Salisbury. Also to report on the possibilities of large-scale development of ship-building in the area and the potential of Christchurch harbour for providing suitable anchorage for ships of the line.

After extensive exploration Yarranton reported back in terms of high optimism on all points. The river could, with ease, be made navigable as far as Salisbury, and the accessibility of vast New Forest timber supplies which could be carried down the river at four shillings per load or tun could create a far more economical industry than was currently in operation at Portsmouth. The harbour at Christchurch could afford accommodation to fifty or sixty fifth and sixth rate frigates, while Hengistbury Head was a natural fortress for the lodgement of 100,000 men. In the end, problems of finance and flooding were too great. Otherwise, a report on the Corporations of England and Wales

14: Afene

submitted to the House of Commons in 1835 might have read differently from:

> *"The town of Christchurch is not a place of such importance or consideration, nor do there appear to be in operation any causes which are likely to produce any great increase of prosperity or population."*

There are several written references to the River Avon's ability to form ground ice, a phenomenon virtually unknown in this country, although shared by the nearby Moors River, a tributary of the Stour. In the great freeze of January 1963 some residents of Sopley recall standing on the frozen waters of the millrace and peering beneath their feet at great balls of ice colliding and cannoning their way along the river bed.

Worship

The two oldest institutions in Sopley village have complemented each other through the centuries in their ministering to people's spiritual and bodily needs. There they stand, the church and the mill, the one overlooking the other in a topographical attempt to establish the right order of precedence. For Sopley Church has its own enigmatic eminence from which to survey its pastures; its tower does not need to be high. On a clear day it can maintain visual contact with its pre-Reformation 'mother', the Priory at Christchurch. And it is through this link with Christchurch-Twynham that Sopley Church first becomes documented.

Before the Norman Conquest much is conjectural. The fact that there is no mention of a church in *Domesday* is not particularly surprising or significant. In 1053 Earl Godwin endowed what was probably a small Saxon chapel with one virgate. Evidence of Saxon places of worship in the Avon Valley is not far to seek; Breamore provides an excellent example.

When the Snow Lay Round About. Sopley Parish Church.
Photograph loaned by Leslie Freeman.

16: Worship

Much speculation has arisen concerning the mound on which the church stands. Was it a pagan temple? Such an idea is not incredible by any means; but proof is difficult to find. Writing in 1933 a Roman Catholic priest posed the following considerations:

> *"May I suggest that the hill on which Sopley Church is situated might lend itself to expert investigation. As it must have been in historical times on tidal waters its evident artificial isolation indicates that before the erection of the church, that is to say before St Aldhelm's evangelisation of the district, it was a sort of naval station for the Jute invaders of the forest area (not to the exclusion of Lymington perhaps but still probably as their chief inlet as it has an open sea approach). More nearly allied to the Danes than to the Angles or Saxons they would build moot hills and use the rivers as their main roads to the interior. The Avon had probably been canalised before this time by the Belgae and the Atrebates. Sopley would be a place high up from the sea, a base for raids on the interior and a site for building their galleys with limitless timber supplies."*

In answer to the view that the church mound is only a continuation of the natural hill on which stands a house called Morden, and that the cutting between them has been caused by centuries of traffic to and from the mill, he commented:

> *"I have no doubt that Sopley's moot or 'thing' is partly natural, but I think it will be found as Caesar said of a British position — it is both art and nature combined."*

At the beginning of his reign in 1100, Henry I granted Twynham to Richard de Redvers, whose son Baldwin became the first Earl of Devon. Through the years members of the de Redvers family issued charters confirming the canons of the Priory in all of their possessions, including Sopley. At first, a charter of 1137 confirms to the Priory Sopley chapel — *"capella de Soppelee"*; a few years later it is referred to as Sopley church — *"ecclesia de Soppelee"*, with all that belongs to it.

Interestingly enough, in the 12th century, the ownership of Sopley church was disputed by the Priory at Breamore. The eagerly awaited publication of the *Christchurch Cartulary* will make possible the reading of the details of this dispute. It was only when Christchurch agreed to pay annually 40lb of pure wax that Breamore dropped its claim. Its Priory must have been particularly

17: Worship

well candle-lit for a while, until a payment of fifteen shillings per annum was substituted. The insistence on the preservation of this obligation suggests that there must have been some legal sympathy for Breamore's 'bogus' claim.

The fact that the dispute between Christchurch and Breamore took place at all is perhaps a lifting of the veil which obscures many disputes in early Norman times over endowments which had occurred before 1066. It was about now that the Anglo-Saxon system of central churches, or minsters, serving large 'parishes' through teams of priests, seems to have begun to give way before the appearance of stone-built local churches with resident vicars, whose powers grew steadily. The transition was lengthy, disputes were common, and the minsters held tenaciously to their dues. One is reminded of the immediate prelude to the most famous of all nativity stories, by a memorandum in the *Christchurch Cartulary*, which notes the obligation that Sopley, together with other 'daughter' churches in the 'parish', must visit their 'mother' church at Christchurch on Ascension Day, or the Sunday following, taking candles varying in size and value according to the number of parishioners. It was the de Stantons who claimed to be the true founders of Sopley church and it was they who 'gave' it to Breamore. Dogged persistence on the part of Dean Hilary eventually won the day for Christchurch. Soon afterwards, the rights of the canons of Christchurch relating to Sopley were commuted for an annual pension of five shillings.

Specific Sopley church information during the Middle Ages is inevitably rather scarce, but again the opening of the *Christchurch Cartulary* will give substance to shadows. It will record the shortcomings of the 14th century vicar, John Herynge, referred to in the church guidebook, and reveal disputes over tithe obligations and kindred problems, perhaps after all not too far removed from the daily round of our modern welfare state.

The oldest part of the church as it stands today is the chancel; but in the eleventh and twelfth centuries the whole building stood within the space that is now occupied by the central nave and the west end with its tower. The present chancel was built on to the old church in the thirteenth century. Then, during the next hundred years the nave was rebuilt, north and south transepts were added, making the building cruciform, and the nave was widened by the provision of north and south aisles.

It is known that by the middle of the nineteenth century the church of St Michael and All Angels was in very urgent need of repair; more of this later. During these earlier years there was no shortage of gifts and bequests; this was fortunate, for in 1280 the Convocation of Canterbury ordered that the parishioners of each parish church within the province should provide the following articles for the service of the church: chalice, missal, principal

Sermons in Stone.
The Church of St Michael and All Angels, Sopley.
Top left, from NE: tower, porch, north transept.
Centre right: view from south; tower, new vestry, south transept.
Bottom left, from NW: tower and porch.
Reproduced by permission of Basil White.

vestments—chasuble, alb, amice, stole, maniple, girdle, two towels, processional cross, lesser cross for the dead, Holy water vestments, pax, Easter candlestick, bells in steeple with ropes, font with lock and key. Later came instructions concerning the provision of compulsory service books etc., and much later (1604) all churches were ordered to have a pulpit. Sopley's pulpit dates from that year, possibly the first to be supplied in the country in direct response to that decree.

A Venetian traveller in England in the 16th century, writing of the wealth of this country, says:

19: Worship

"But above all are their riches displayed in the church treasures, for there is not a parish throughout the land so humble but has its crosses, candlesticks, censers, basins (i.e. patens) and cups of silver (boccali d'argento)."

A local 16th century will, in the name of Joan Tulse, who died in 1533 reveals the following bequests to Sopley church:

"to the high altar – 12d.
to repairing the church of Sopley – a cow.
to the sepulchre of light – a bushel of barley
to the crown light – 4d.
to the image of St Catherine – an kerchief
another to St Margaret.
to the image of Our Lady in the fields – a pair of beads
to the vicary – 6s. 8d.
to the light of St Nicholas – 5d.
to dressing of rood and crucifix over chancel door – 3s. 4d.

Two inventories of church valuables were ordered to be made in the troubled years of the reign of the youthful Edward VI, the second one in 1552. Special commissioners for this purpose were appointed for Hampshire, who were: Marquis of Winchester, Sir Richard Cotton, Sir Henry Seymour, Sir Richard Wingfield, William Kellaway, Richard Worsey and John Kingsmill. Their instructions included:

"And if ye shall find any person or persons that wilfully refuse to obey any precept or commandment which you our said commissioners, four or three of you, shall give unto them in or about the execution of the premises, that then we give unto you full power and authority to commit every such person to ward or prison, there to remain without bail or mainprise, until such time as you shall think, and same imprisonment to be condign for his or their offences."

The second inventory lists the following items: a chalice of silver with a patine; a payre of blew vestments of velvet; a pair of white damaske vestements; a pair of vestments of grine bawdkin; *ij* payre of grine vestements; *j* cope of bawdkin; *ij* alter clothes of linen; a payre of orgaynes; *iiij* belles hanging in the stepell; *ij* tinne candalstikes; one holy water pot; Latine

20: Worship

candalstikes; a Latine cross; *iij* cofers; towelles of linen; one lampe of brase; *ij* surplicis and a rochet.

Then comes the statement that the following items have been "stolene oute of the sayd churche since the last inventory in 1549": one payre of blewe damaske vestments; one cope of bawdkin and one alter clothe of Satin a Brigis; Latine basons and one Latine cross; one holiwater potte; *j* payre of whit vestments of Baudkin.

This whole document is signed by Franciscus Baknall, Vicar, churchwardens John Edmonds and Edward Kyng, and sidemen John Ginking and Nicholas Parker.

The career of the Vicar, Francis Bucknall, must have included vicissitudes of fortune, alarms and excursions, heart-searchings and anguish, familiar to many in those fraught days. It seems probable that he was one of the Christchurch Canons driven out at the dissolution of the Priory in 1539. It is recorded that during Edward VI's reign he was taken to London and imprisoned in the Marshalsea, where he was not allowed communication with anyone without the express consent of the Lords of the Privy Council. His imprisonment had nothing to do with the disappearance of valuables from the church; it was possibly due to his failure to use the second new version of Cranmer's Prayer Book issued in 1549. It is known that he became a monk again during Mary's brief return to Rome. Those days were riddled with suspicion and intrigue. In 1552 a letter was sent to the Lord Chancellor to make out a Commission of Oyer and Terminer to be made out to such gentlemen of Hampshire as he shall think mete for that purpose for the examination of a conspiracy by dyvers lewd personnes there...

Between the Reformation and the great restoration of Sopley church in 1868, the thread of continuity is sometimes a little difficult to trace. For a time biographical details of succeeding vicars, which have been admirably recorded in the church's official handbook, maintain the story. Thomas Brooke carried the church from Tudor into Stuart days, and despite a fine newly-installed pulpit he was summoned before the Bishop's court for neglect of 'divine service and sermons'. Midway through the reign of James I, Vicar John Hilliard wrote a tract called *Fire from Heaven*, including an account of a much-publicised supernatural occurrence in the neighbouring village of Holdenhurst. Thomas Lake 'presided' at Sopley during the Stuart civil war; he was much bolder in the publicising of his Royalist sympathies than a nearby Sussex vicar, who tried to salve his conscience by singing a variation of the last verse of the *Te Deum* each Sunday morning, having first insured that his voice would be drowned by others: "O Lord in Thee have I trusted, let me never be a Roundhead."

21: Worship

For approximately one hundred years the names of Sopley vicars are 'naked'. Early in the 18th century however the Manor of Sopley and the advowson of the church were bought by James Willis of Ringwood. His younger son and grandson, both James, ministered in Sopley from 1746-1835, with a gap of nine years early on. Each was an 18th century squarson, combining the rôles of squire and parson. James Willis II, who was instituted in 1779, was prominent in the popularising of Merino sheep breeding in the Avon Valley and in 1810 a treatise on this subject was published and dedicated to him. He remained Vicar of Sopley until his death in 1835, though during his closing years parish affairs were ably and vigorously managed by the curate, William Douglas Veitch. Veitch was in Sopley for a few years only, leaving in 1841, but such was the regard in which he was held that when he died, over forty years later, a large church window was dedicated to his memory. He had a daughter named Zepherina Philadelphia, who became known as "the Florence Nightingale of mid-wives".

In 1866 William Henry Lucas was appointed vicar. It fell to him to organise a massive repair programme at the church, particularly the chancel, following a sombre and ominous report on the state of the building by the Archdeacon of Winchester.

The needed sum of six hundred pounds for interior work was raised through the efforts of many; the Lay Rectors who were members of the Wyndham family, met the cost of their responsibility for chancel work. As the result of a magnificent combined effort, the church was given a 'new look' and emerged very much as it is today. The original faculty for all this, issued on 26th October 1867, read as follows:

> *"to remove and replace in other positions in said church, the said pulpit, reading desk and other fittings according to the said plans approved by us, and also to take down and remove all such ornaments and mural tablets as it may be found necessary or desirable to take down and remove in carrying out the said work provided that such monuments and mural tablets be replaced in the same situation from which same may be removed, or as near thereto as circumstances will permit."*

A few hidden delights from the past were uncovered, notably the Early English lancet windows in the chancel, and the wooden roofing in the nave. Two windows above the chancel arch were covered in.

This was local dedication and perseverance at its best, the embodiment of a pride in local fellowship which inspires great works. Complacency has no part

22: Worship

in the preservation of hallowed treasures and the challenge is a permanent one. A great storm in 1893 did huge damage to the roof. There was no money left for the tower in 1868, and the problem of strengthening it and recasting the bells had to be faced in the 1920s. In more recent times, further extensive repair work has been carried out, notably on the great west window which supplies Sopley Church with much of its natural light.

Gifts of new treasures were not for ever stifled by Puritan zeal. Many gifts are related to thanksgiving, many to commemoration, and many to uncomplicated devotion. There are stained-glass windows, most of them not very old, and the organ, the gift of a member of a fourth generation of Sopley Willises, General Sir George Harry Smith Willis; memorials to the dead of two world wars, the oak doors to the north and south in memory of two faithful churchwardens, an embroidered collage depicting the life of Sopley Village in 1984, assembled by ladies of the parish at the time of a Festival of Flowers. A treble bell was added to the existing peal of five in 1963.

To the north of the village a cemetery was opened in 1895 and the churchyard has been closed to burials since the beginning of the 20th century. Although many of the gravestones are weather-beaten in an obliterated kind of way, they stand in their rows under the wings of the building where the departed communed. On one of them, marking the grave of Moses Grove, who died in 1817, are the words:

> *"Here lies a father who on earth*
> *Was neither rich nor poor,*
> *But what he left surpassed in worth*
> *A nobleman's estate.*
> *To all who knew him it was given,*
> *And is a fortune ample,*
> *Rather than house or lands, thank Heaven,*
> *It was a good example."*

In the chapter on Sopley schools it will be seen that for a long time separate provision was made for the education of Nonconformist children on the one hand and Church of England on the other. Towards the close of the 18th century the Rev. W. Hopkins became Pastor of Christchurch Congregational Church, and in conjunction with the Rev. Alfred Bishop, Independent Minister at Ringwood, he undertook to take responsibility for services to be held at a house in Ripley called Towns End. A succeeding Christchurch pastor, Rev. Daniel Gunn, assumed responsibility for Ripley and the mission was transferred from Towns End to the house of Mr Benjamin Tuck. This site soon

23: Worship

became far too small, and Mr Tuck's garden was offered as a site for a chapel. Four hundred pounds was raised and building began.

The new chapel, capable of seating a large congregation, was opened in 1822, and it became a distinct Congregational Church in 1829, Mr Gunn recommending that all who lived north of Winkton should attend Ripley. In the decades that followed, relationships between church and chapel were often strained and mistrust was mutual. A penny paper of large circulation and dissenting principles in the Christchurch area, called *The Christian World*, published the following news item:

> "*We may mention that at Sopley Harvest Festival there was, in the morning, a full choral service and in the afternoon, in the field adjoining the Vicarage, races were held, including one by "young women" aged 28-30 and one by wives and widows only. Such is ritualism!*"

This called forth the following retort from Vicar Lucas at Sopley:

> "*It is true that a neighbouring farmer, noted by the bye for his strong opposition to ritualism in any shape, proposed that such races should take place. It is also true to say that, on the remonstrance of others, those races were at once abandoned.*"

The vicar received an apology in due course.

Succeeding pastors at Ripley must have been encouraged by the size of their congregations. Their names were: Charles Thurman; William Hopkins; J. Locke (became a missionary in S. Africa 1837); Alfred Newth; R.R. Davies; R. Davey; Francis Baron; F.W. Turner (became a missionary in British Guiana); H. Waring; L.J. Bailey; G.E. Page; R. Howarth 1901-1939.

In 1880 the chapel was rebuilt by John Kemp-Welch and it remained in that form until its very recent demolition. The centenary of the church was celebrated in devotion and in style in 1929 and it is noteworthy of the continuity of local life in earlier days that when the Ripley Sunday School anniversary service was held in 1957, three generations of the same family took the collection.

Life in Ripley was at one time regularly enlivened by visits from the Salvation Army who took services round a large elm tree which was known as the Hallelujah tree.

A fairly large number of Roman Catholics continued to live locally after the Reformation despite persecution of varying degrees of diligence. Some

24: Worship

were buried in the churchyard. One particularly interesting gravestone within the church, in front of the pulpit, is that of Elizabeth Perkins, the second wife of Edmund Perkins, who came of an old Roman Catholic family and lived at Winkton. Elizabeth died in 1693, and it is of considerable historical interest that in 1694 her husband became one of two guardians and tutors to Prince James Edward, the Old Pretender. Edmund was held in great esteem by all around him; he died in Paris in 1697. Another tombstone with a Latin inscription which strongly suggests a Roman Catholic connection, lies in front of the lectern. It records the burial of Maria, wife of Mark Ford, who died on 6th June 1699, aged 35.

Tradition suggests that the Roman Catholics of the local community used to worship at Springfield House, Avon, opposite to Court House and Farm belonging to the Fane family. Within the living memory of some who were alive a hundred years ago, a font was in a room close to the river.

In Sopley village there is Priest Lane, and at the end of it is Priest House, where the local Roman Catholic priest used to live. On December 21st 1765 the priest's home caught fire and the priest (Rev. Flanagan) perished in the ensuing blaze. He appears to have come downstairs and when near ground level a beam fell upon him and killed him. The house was not rebuilt for some time, and during this time Catholics went to Mass at Stapehill or Canford House.

When the house was rebuilt, Rev. Parker was the first priest to live there. He was succeeded by Rev. Greening who lived in Sopley for a while but eventually moved to Christchurch. The tragic circumstances surrounding his death are recorded in another chapter. He was succeeded by Rev. Beni, a French priest, and Rev. Chantittour who lodged with Mr Juno Godden, coachman to Mr Walcott of Winkton.

For a brief while the Stapehill nuns with their supervisor, Madame Chaban, came to live at Burton House, having been driven from France. They were followed at Burton House by Sir Thomas More, with Lady Mannock, his niece. Sir Thomas's priest, Rev. Vial, said Mass at Sopley. Next on the scene was a French migrant priest, Rev. Cochet, who came to Sopley from Stapehill on Sundays and Holy days. With the assistance of Lady Mannock, M. Cochet purchased a house and garden at Burton Green and this became the site of the Chapel House. The building of the chapel was begun in 1810, and opened by Bishop Poynter in 1811. Rev. Cochet suffered with paralysis; he retired to France where he recovered and died in 1830. Lady Mannock died at Endless Street, Salisbury, leaving in her will £800 for the mission at Sopley. Today, the nearest Roman Catholic centre of worship to Sopley is at Purewell; the 19th century Roman Catholic chapel on Burton Green is now the local home of the United Reformed Church.

SOPLEY PARISH CHURCH OF ST MICHAEL AND ALL ANGELS

List of Known Vicars. Earlier dates do not necessarily coincide with dates of institution.

1308	William de Broctone.	1317	Richard de Hortune.
1324	Nicholas de Weston.	1347	John Herynge.
1396	John Churchehay.	1453	John Dorneford.
1453	John Coverdale.	1457	John Homyngton.
1471	John Wheler.	1471	John Ray.
1493	John Pope.	1529	Richard Good.
1540	Francis Bucknall.	1557	William Clerke.
1558	William Ryeland.	1568	Thomas Kyndge.
1575	Thomas Brooke.	1613	John Hilliard.
1634	Thomas Lake.	1652	J. Walker.
1661	Thomas Muspratt.	1674	James Bampton.
1676	Maurice Edwards.	1689	Thomas Ansty.
1691	Thomas Stephens.	1728	Henry Derby.
1740	Westbrooke Singer.	1746	James Willis I.
1770	Harry Place.	1779	James Willis II.
1835	John P Hammond.	1866	William H Lucas.
1888	James F Vallings.	1929	David F Wright.
1942	Charles D Kirkham.	1967	Percy O Sandercombe.
	1973	Alan Sessford.	

26: Worship

Advowson and the Descent of the Lay Rectory of Sopley After the Dissolution of the Larger Monasteries in 1539.

Sopley Church continued to be appropriated to Christchurch and to receive vicars appointed by the Prior and canons until the dissolution of the Priory in 1539. The original dedication of the Church of St Michael the Archangel was changed after the Reformation to St Michael and All Angels.

Lay Rectors.

- 1539 Thomas Wriothesley and William Avery.
- 1548 Robert Whight.
- 1600*c*. Sir William Webbe.
- 1627 Sir John Cooke and Rachel his wife (d. of Sir W. Webbe).
- 1646 The rectory was sequestered as a result of John Cooke Junior's adherence to the Royalist cause. He was ordered to pay £80 yearly out of the profits by the Committee of Plundered Ministers.
- 1705 Rectory conveyed to George Wyndham and this Wiltshire family still owned it in 1849 when the great tithes were commuted for £580 and the vicarial tithes for £330.
  The present lectern in the church was given in memory of Thomas Wyndham who died in 1881.
- 1870*c*. The advowson of Sopley Church was bought by a member of the Lucas family.
- 1874 An Order in Council, dated 28th January, decreed an exchange whereby Charles Thomas Lucas became patron of Warnham in Sussex and the Dean and Chapter of Canterbury became patrons of Sopley.

Note: from time to time during the latter part of the 19th century and the early part of the 20th century, there was correspondence concerning the rector's liability for the upkeep of the chancel. Eventually, a letter from the Diocesan Board of Finance confirmed that the liability for the upkeep of the chancel passed from the lay rector to the Parochial Church Council when tithes were finally extinguished in 1936.

The Vicarage, Sopley.
Photograph loaned by May Mould.

Footnote

Extracts from correspondence concerning the possible purchase of the advowson in the second half of the 19th century.

a). Two references to the Vicarage:

> *"There is a new substantial dwelling house, with offices, garden and premises, together with 30 acres of glebe."* (20th April 1867).

> *"I have almost rebuilt this house and restored the church and find myself quite settled there."* (Letter circa 1870).

b). Two references to the Parish:

> *"Moreover he (the client) has an impression that the Parish and neighbourhood is not very desirable."* (October 1870).

> *"I have visited Sopley and find that nearly all the inhabitants, including the squire, are Dissenters. I am willing to buy the advowson, subject to title, but I need time."* (1st June 1871).

28: Worship

Marriages at Sopley Church 1682-1812

A total of 694 marriages during a period of 130 years are recorded: the late 17th century records are not complete, but it can be assessed with reasonable accuracy that there were, on average, 5-6 marriages a year during this time.

It may come as a surprise to discover the number of brides or grooms who, in those very parochial days, came from comparatively far afield. In 355 (about half) of the marriages being considered, both bride and groom lived in Sopley. As might be anticipated, a large number (187) hailed from Christchurch, and some 62 from Ringwood. The following place names occur from twice to ten times: Holdenhurst, Milton, Lymington, Wimborne, Cranborne, Hordle, Fordingbridge, Hampreston, Milford, Boldre, Ellingham, Salisbury, Poole, Burley, Chippenham, Brockenhurst, Damerham, Embury, Horton, Romsey. 57 place names occur once during these years, including towns and villages in Devon, the Isle of Wight, Yorkshire, Cheshire, Sussex, Herts, Guernsey.

88 of these marriage entries include mention of marriage licences. Licences to dispense with the necessity of banns have been granted by bishops since the 14th century, a power confirmed to them by Peter's Pence Act in 1534 (25 H VIII c.21).

From 1769 "sojourners" appear in the marriage lists. Could it be that Sopley's tourist trade dates from about this time?

Occupations are seldom recorded but mentioned are: schoolmaster, mason, dyer, salt officer (Isle of Wight). Occasionally, one of the partners is listed as a pauper, and some minors are revealed, usually female, but sometimes male. Could the latter be the lifting of the corner of the curtain on 'shot-gun' marriages?

Among bridegrooms' names, popularity is shared between William, John, Thomas, Richard and Joseph. Elizabeth and Mary are easily the most frequently occurring brides' names, while an unusual and picturesque name for a bride, in 1759, is Monimia.

About half way through the period of time under consideration – 1798 – there were 22 christenings and baptisms, six marriages, and 18 burials, a pattern that exists throughout with comparatively little variation, chiefly a reduction in the number of baptisms.

Sopley Charities

Brown's Charity. In 1667 Thomas Brown, Esq., of Hinton Admiral, left lands and goods for charitable uses in the parishes of Christchurch, Ringwood, Lymington, Minstead, Milton, Holdenhurst, Lyndhurst, and Sopley. Sopley was to receive three pounds and ten shillings for the distribution of bread, groceries and clothing on New Year's Day; these gifts were later provided in cash. The Vicar was to receive ten shillings for the annual preaching on New Year's Day of a sermon on "Man's misery in his natural condition and of our reconciliation to God by the Lord Jesus Christ".

Edward Elliott. In 1677 he bequeathed ten shillings per annum to provide bread to be set on a table in the church for the poor and the aged who have been "at the prayers and sermon".

Sir Henry Tulse. Lord Mayor of London in 1684 (and probable descendant of the Joan Tulse whose Tudor will has been noted elsewhere) left one hundred pounds to the poor of Sopley.

Thomas Bemister Tizzard. In 1712 he left twenty shillings for the poor and ten shillings "to a godly minister" for preaching a sermon on Holy Thursday.

John Tuck. In 1860 he bequeathed the interest on £110 19s. 7d. for "Christmas comforts".

Sir George Willis. In 1901 he left money for the upkeep of the family monuments; any money left over should be used for suitable charitable purposes.

NOTE. **Tulse and Brown Charities.** Children were given 9d or 10d each on New Year's Day on condition that the money was spent either in the shop at Sopley, or at Winkton.

The Manor of Sopley

before A.D. 1066. *held by Edric.*
1086. *held by William son of Stur.*
1263. *John de Bockhampton held one knight's fee in Sopley of Baldwin, E. of Devon. Roger de Stanton held 1 knight's fee (manor held of Lords of Christchurch Manor).*
1276. *John, son of John. Brother Robert succeeds.*

1297. *held after Robert's death by 4th sister Joan, wife of Theobald Butler (le Botiller).*	1287. *one moiety to Sir Henry le Moyne.*
1303. *Joan dies, son Edward succeeds.*	
1316. *Edward Butler.*	1316. *Joan. Widow of Sir Henry.*
1321. *James (son of Edward). 1st Earl of Ormonde.*	
1337. *succeeded by widow Eleanor and son James, a minor – El. M. Thomas, Lord Dagworth.*	
1346. *son James succeeds – 2nd Earl of Ormonde.*	1346. *Robert Selyman & Sir H. le Moyne, grandson of 1st Sir Henry.*
1382. *son James. 3rd E. of Ormonde.*	1376. *to sons Henry & William.*
1405. *James succeeds.*	1397. *William owns it.*
1428. *James.*	1414. *to nephew John.*
1503. *Thomas. 7th E. of Ormonde.*	1428c. *died; to Elizabeth (daughter). She married William Stourton.*
1515. *to d. Lady Anne de Leger.*	
1533. *son, Sir George de Leger.*	1431. *then to Abarowe family until*
1575. *he or son sold it to Sir John Berkeley Kt.*	1544. *sold to Sir William Berkeley Kt.*
	1551. *son Sir John Berkeley.*

1575. *Sir John Berkeley holds both moieties of the manor and conveys to William Waller.*
1603. *William sells to brother John Waller.*
1619. *J. Waller died. Manor settled on niece Susan and her husband, Sir Richard Tichborne Kt.*
1689. *son, Sir Henry Tichborne owned manor.*
1725c. *Sir Henry sold to James Willis.*
1753. *manor passed to nephew John Compton from whom it passed, like Minstead, to Henry Francis Compton in early 19th century.*

Domesday and Beyond

The Sopley entry in the Hampshire Domesday.

The seeking out of early documents relating to the Sopley area involves a fair share of puzzles and problems. Frequent references to the hundred, the tithing, and the manor, make it necessary to have at least a little knowledge of the significance of these names.

Hundreds were territorial divisions, which as early as the 11th century, were the heart of public justice and finance throughout Southern England. In some parts of the country hundreds approximated to a round 100 hides but in others the hundred varied widely between 20 and 150 hides.

Shortly before the Norman Conquest each hundred had its court which dealt with such things as thieves and those who were slow in their pursuit, and decided disputes between individual taxpayers and the Crown. The court met every month in the open air and must have looked very much like the old folk moots.

In early Medieval times, hundreds were joined financially to ancient royal manors, and it seems reasonable to assume that profits arising from their dispensations formed part of the manor's revenue.

The word *manerium* is not easy to define, and the estates involved varied tremendously. Often the area covered by one manor could be a large part of a county, and could include a number of villages; others could be very small and sometimes a village might be divided between several different manors.

The word *tithing* too had numerical origins, involving a group of ten householders. It was basically a tenth of a hundred and therefore was as varied in content as the hundred itself. Ancient boundaries in a given area were very often a complicated mixture of hundreds, tithings, and later, parishes (civil and ecclesiastical).

At the time of *Domesday* in 1086 the Manor of Sopley was in the Hundred of Sirlie or Shirley together with five others – two at Avene (Avon), two at Ripley and one at Weringtone (Winkton). A translation of the *Domesday* entry relating to Sopley reads:

> "*William son of Stur holds Sopelie. Edric held it of King Edward as an alod* (in alodium*). It then paid geld for seven hides: now for one hide and half a virgate. There is land for two ploughs. In (the demesne) is one plough; and (there are) three villeins and six bordars with two ploughs. There is one serf and a mill worth ten shillings and 875 eels and 59 acres of meadow. T.R.E. it was worth ten pounds and afterwards ten shillings; (it is) now (worth) 50 shillings but it pays 100 shillings. The king has four hides of this manor and all the woodland (*nemus*) in his forest. The whole of this is worth 110 shillings.*"

There are also *Domesday* entries in similar style for the two manors of Avon (one assessed at 8 hides and one at one hide) and two manors of Ripley (two hides and half a hide).

A few definitions may contribute to a fuller appreciation of the substance of the Sopley entry. *Alod* or *alodium* was the term used for land held in absolute ownership. William, son of Stur, was an extensive land owner, particularly in the Isle of Wight. *Geld* means tax. The *hide* was essentially a unit of tax assessment, varying in magnitude from sixty to over one hundred acres. A *virgate* was usually about thirty acres. A *villein* was a peasant personally bound to his lord to whom he paid dues and services; a *bordar* was a small freeholder. Commonly, *Domesday* entries bore frequent reference to statistics prevailing immediately before the Conquest as well as the contemporary situation. T.R.E. was the recognised abbreviation for *Tempore Regis Edwardi* – in the time of King Edward; T.R.W. – *Tempore Regis Willelmi* – in the time of King William.

Shirley Hundred, consisting of Sopley, Ripley, Avon and Winkton, corresponded fairly closely to the Parish of Sopley, and here it should be noted that there have never been great variations between the civil and ecclesiastic boundaries of Sopley Parish. Shirley (or Sirlie) Hundred was still existing separately in 1176 but by the middle of the 13th century it had been absorbed into the Parish of Holdenhurst, which at this time included the whole of the modern Hundred of Christchurch with Westover Liberty. By the early years of the 14th century the Hundred of Shirley seems to have come into the Hundred of Christchurch which was divided as follows: the upper half contained Boldre, Hordle, Milford and Milton; the lower half contained that part of Christchurch which was outside the old borough, together with the Parish of Sopley. This lower half is often referred to as Christchurch Foreign, or the

Outhundred of Christchurch. There were separate hundred courts held for separate districts of the Borough of Christchurch as early as 1500, and confirmation is found of the existence of four tithings in the Parish of Sopley, namely: Sopley, Avon, Ripley and Shirley. The last three lay roughly within the Manor of Avon Tyrell, and the tithing of Sopley appears to have come within the Manor of Sopley.

The list of the Lords of the Manor of Sopley is an impressive one but in the early years after the Norman Conquest there is little or no evidence of a resident lord or of any personal impact upon the life of the local community. A glance at the list will reveal that a second Manor of Sopley (a moiety) was created about 1287, each moiety being held as a quarter of a knight's fee. This moiety remained separate until 1551 when the two moieties were owned together by Sir John Berkeley and from that time followed the same descent.

Several Sopley Lords of the Manor achieved fame on the national stage. This was particularly true of the Butler family who were in possession of the manor from 1297 until early Tudor times. For example, Thomas Butler, the seventh Earl of Ormonde, served under Richard III and Henry VII as ambassador to France and Burgundy, and his elder brother, Sir John, ambassador to many European countries, was described by Edward IV as "the goodliest knight I ever beheld and the first gentleman in Christendom". There is now virtually no trace of Sopley Manor records (neighbouring Avon is more fortunate in this respect). Today the almost entirely titular lord of the manor is difficult to trace, by so much has his old power and prestige vanished from the English scene.

It seems likely that during the medieval centuries listed in the tree of manorial descent the lives of the ordinary people of Sopley were often touched by the proximity of the New Forest, and inevitably by the taxman. There is no good reason for believing, however, that Sopley was at one time included in the boundaries of the New Forest. In 1789, the government Fifth Forest Report writes of the western boundary as being from the bridge at Christchurch, up the River Avon as far as the bridge at Fordingbridge. A superficial glance at the Sopley *Domesday* entry would seem to indicate that the manor, or part of it, was included within the boundaries: "the king has four hides of this manor and all the woodland (*nemus*) in his forest." Local historian A.T. Lloyd has argued the strong likelihood that this would mean land subject to forest law, rather than an integral part of the New Forest. His researches certainly seem to indicate that where *Domesday* has the heading *"the New Forest and round about it"*, Sopley belongs to the latter half of this description. Reference to the so-called Laws of Canute of 1016 to prove the existence of the New Forest before the Conquest should be treated with caution. It seems that Cnut (Canute) was responsible for only one authentic

34: Domesday and Beyond

forest law; it states:

> "Everyone is to avoid trespassing on my hunting ground wherever I wish to have it preserved, on payment of full fine."

No forest is named.

The publication of the activities of the New Forest courts makes fascinating reading and in 1296 we find the name of John Michel of Sopley listed as a pledge for 'those in mercy' in a deer-poaching case in which the Vicar of Boldre was actively involved.

The question of New Forest boundaries was very important to ordinary men and women, for the rules and penalties which Norman kings imposed on local inhabitants were formidable. Yet the New Forest legislation, designed for the protection of the king's deer, never interfered with the process of common law and there seems to be no evidence of New Forest Courts invading the bounds of common justice administered by the shire and hundred courts.

The cost of government and methods of meeting this cost will never be far away from the centre of the political arena. Tax assessments called Tenths and Fifteenths, calculated on the value of a person's moveable goods, including crops, was at the heart of the system. Later, fixed sums were substituted for different areas. By Tudor times it was found necessary to introduce subsidies, which were based on a yield of 2s 8d on goods and four shillings in the pound on land. A very heavy tax was authorised in 1585, in the face of growing threats from Spain and its Armada and elaborate arrangements were drawn up for its collection. The returns for Sopley were:

Goods:		
Elizabeth Donestone	_	£7 7s 0d;
Alice Hopkins	_	£5 5s 0d;
William Potter	_	£4 4s 0d;
Richard Moyle	_	£3 3s 0d;
Joan Wendover	_	£3 3s 0d;
Nicholas Norris	_	£5 5s 0d;
Thomas Eliot	_	£3 3s 0d;
John Sebut	_	£3 3s 0d;
Thomas Wendover	_	£5 5s 0d;
Martin Saunders	_	£3 3s 0d;
George Bate	_	£3 3s 0d.

The above tax details come from *The Hampshire Lay Subsidy Rolls, 1586*, edited by C.R. Davey, return no. 337 for Sopley, published by HCC, 1981.

The Miller's Tale

Next to the church, both physically and in terms of the importance of continuity, stands Sopley Mill. It is a very large building, much enlarged and altered in 1878, which dominates utterly the spot upon which it stands; yet it is encountered very suddenly below the churchyard wall and can easily be missed by a casual visitor to the village.

The mill-stream waters, which for hundreds of years drove the under-shot water wheel and then the water turbine which replaced it late in the 19th century, divert from the main river half a mile or so upstream, at a point known as Wild Weirs. This valley is full of evocative names such as this. Close by is 'Dismal Swamp' and these two names alone produce a Thomas Hardy-born atmosphere that is ghostly and seems far removed from the nearby endless procession of twentieth century automation. The mill stream rejoins its parent a short distance below the mill, the River Avon seemingly flowing back on its tracks in order to reclaim its offspring.

It is difficult to overemphasise the importance of the water mills in the lives of our ancestors. Literature has contrived a traditional picture of the miller, round-faced and jovial, earthy and earthly, and full of the business 'acumen' reflected in the origins of the rôle in transactions of the miller's thumb. Sopley mill is picturesquely recorded in *Domesday*, whereas Sopley Church is not mentioned. Its annual payment of ten shillings and eight hundred and seventy-five eels occasions great interest to this day.

Domesday makes no mention of Avon Mill, yet it and possibly two others existed in the parish in medieval times; ancient references to these mills do not always make it clear which mill is being referred to. Avon Mill as such must have ceased to function by the time of the nineteenth century Commutation of Tithes; as late as 1957 one of its mill-stones was dredged from the river and is now in a quiet corner of Wiltshire.

But to return to Sopley Mill. It is known that in 1725 it was owned and/or occupied by a Thomas Brenton, whose marriage to Mary Hayward on Guy Fawkes Day in 1699 is recorded in the parish registers. By 1754 it was owned by Thomas' son and heir, William. The Brenton family appear to have owned Sopley and Avon Mills throughout the bulk of the 18th century, although a William Ward, in his will dated 1747, is described as "of Sopley, Miller".

A record of 1822 notes that in this year Mr George Olive Aldridge of Christchurch purchased of Mr John Bound the fee simple of an ancient cornmill and premises thereto belonging situate on a branch of the River Avon at Sopley. At about this time Mr Aldridge acquired Sopley Farm and owned it until is death in 1882. Apparently Mr Aldridge never lived in Sopley. He owned property also in Winkton and started brewery and wine businesses in Christchurch and Poole.

It seems that wherever there were several corn mills in a comparatively limited stretch of the same river, there were accompanying problems of water flow control. Sopley Mill certainly had its 19th century share of difficulty. Indeed the river valley seems to have excited a long saga of dispute and discontent, relating not only to the supply of water and flooding difficulties, but also fishing rights, boundaries separating the Jocktrill Commons from adjacent estate properties, disturbance of pheasants, trespass, etc. The owner of the mill owned the fishing over the whole of the mill stream and over parts of the main river; he also had an agreement with the Avon Tyrell Estate to take water at the main river along the big ditch leading to Jocktrill, by joining the ditch to the river below Court Farm, and also to throw three wings into the main river at Sharphams, to guide extra water into the mill stream. There was a ford at the north end of Jocktrill leading to the meadow gate and to Sharphams.

By 1878 the mill was owned by F.W. Bemister and he was still in possession in 1899. He added an upper storey to the mill for corn storage and replaced the water wheel by a 12 horse power turbine.

Sopley Mill was a roller mill. There was one 3' 6" wheat store and two barley stores of 4'. The turbine was worked with a 3' 6" fall and was handicapped by short water for 2-3 months per year. The pin level at the mill is O D 18.99.

The undershot water wheel drove a main vertical shaft via bevel gears. This operated three millstone drives from below and a horizontal long shaft which serviced machinery on the first floor via a number of belt drives. When the water wheel was removed a vertical turbine was installed on the south side of the building and was connected to a lower shaft via a long belt drive. One pair of millstones was removed, leaving two pairs still situated at first floor level.

The millers at Sopley Mill in 1911 were J.M. Tinsley and Sons. They worked it as a flour mill until 1914, and it continued as a grist mill until 1946, first under the direction of William Tuck and then, until his death in 1946, by George Cranton. A small amount of wholemeal flour was ground as long as he lived there. Today, plans are developing, both for the preservation of part of the old mill workings on site, and for new projects not necessarily related to the thousand years of activity which have gone before.

37: The Miller's Tale

Inventory and Valuation of Machinery at Sopley Flour Mill. 1881.

(From the Red House Museum Archive in the Dorset Record Office. Ref D546/4195)

Landlord's Property

One single flue Cornish Boiler 4ft × 12ft as fixed, with water gauge and cocks, blow off valve and starting cock.

One six horse power verticle engine – single cylinder. Fly wheel 7' 6" – 14" stroke, 8" diameter, with pulley 35" × 5".

One pair of wood and iron spur wheels, 2" pitch, 66 and 44 cogs respectively 3¾" wide.

One pair of bevel wheels 78 wood cogs, 25 iron cogs, 2" pitch. One counter shaft 3' × 4^3/$_8$". Two plummer blocks, one iron bridge, one iron stone bridge rising gear, stove spindle, cover, neck box, driving irons, pinion fork.

One pair 4ft stones (very inferior), 4ft hoop, wood box, hopper and bin.

Groundshot waterwheel about 11' × 8', wood shaft, wood starts and floats, iron stayed. Gunmetal bearings in wood dog's-hatch and drawing gear complete as fixed.

One 7' mortice iron pit wheel, 70 cogs 3½" pitch. Iron crown head, 36 teeth, 3½" pitch. Arch iron on wood sills and wood upright shaft. Spur wheel and three pinions fitted with segments. Three spindles, 3' 6" neck boxes and driving irons.

Three improved bridges.

One pair of 4' peak stones and one spare pair.

Two pairs of 3' 10" French stones.

Three wood hoops, hoppers and bins.

Exhaust fitted to two pairs of stoves. No. 2 one-sided fan. Pinion and fly wheel.

Twenty-one feet of 2^1/$_8$" fly shafting with sliding clutch.

Four crooked carriages and uprights.

Series of pulleys, bored, turned, and filled with keys.

One set of self-acting hoist tackle complete.

Total value of Landlord's Property: £441 4s 6d.
Munden, Armfield & Co.
Ringwood.

38: The Miller's Tale

Tenant's Property

One malt mill No. 1 size, complete with driven pulley 21" × 14".
One Beam Mill, by Picksly and Sims with driven pulleys 12".
One three wire Grist machine, 10½" cylinders with feed hopper in short case.
One Ashley's Verticle Smither as fixed with dust room, casing upright, driving shaft 2' long with foot box pulleys of 9" × 18", plummer, block and brasses.
Three wheat sevens.
One pair 6" vice on block.
One Munden's silk flour dressing mill and barrel in deal case 21' long with hopper and curbs, iron surveyor, and Swiss silk covering complete.
One Munden's No. 1 Bran duster and combined separator with shoots.
One set of meal elevators, 6" × 5" pulley rollers and slide shoots.
One 8' binslift.
One line of lay shafting 38' × 1^5/$_8$" diameter, with one pair of bright face couplings, 4 plummer blocks fitted with gun metal bearings and lubricators, 3 wood hangers and one wood plate as well.
One intermediate lay shaft 3' × 1¼" diameter, 2 gun metal bearings on wood hangers.
One pair small iron mitre wheels unpitched.
Cast iron pulleys of various widths and diameters.
One set of wheat elevators 12" × 5". 38' lift with iron cups and rubber belt.
132ft of twisted hoist chain.
3 chain pulleys as fixed for hoist tackle.
One set of metal elevators 12" × 5" with 24' lift.
One grindstone on spindle with pulley and handle.
One Munden mixer with 12" and 14" pulley.
450ft of single leather belting, widths varying between 2" and 5".

Total value of Tenant's Property at Sopley Mill: £223 0s 2d.

Munden, Armfield & Co.,
Millwrights & Engineers' Valuers,
Vale of Avon Ironworks, Hants.
26 / 4 / 1881.

The Old Granary, Derritt Lane.
Photograph loaned by Tony Pascoe.

Avon Valley country.
Part of the Mill Stream below Sopley Mill.
Photograph by the author.

Sopley Manor Farm House (demolished)
The river, the Priory, and Hengistbury Head may be seen in the distance.
A reproduction loaned by Basil White.

A view of Quamp.
From left to right in background: The Carpenter's Yard, Well Cottage, Nos. 18, 17, 16.
Photograph loaned by Derek Slade.

The Squire's Tale

Although the ownership of the Manor of Sopley, of which Sopley Park was to become so prominent a part, is traceable to a time before the Norman Conquest, it is only from the early 18th century onwards that written records of the property involved begin to assume detailed proportions. There is a brief record of a deed dated 19th March 1699 between Henry Tichborne and Richard Sanders of Sopley, leasing property for the lives of Richard, his wife, and John Trim, son of Thomas Trim of Christchurch, tallow chandler. The details of the property were the same as those given in a release between Henry Tichborne, of Tichborne, County of Southampton, baronet, and John Brent of Burton in Christchurch Twyneham, Yeoman, dated 10th March 1701. *(From the Tichborne/Brent Agreement 1701 (ref: D/783/T48) at the County Record Office, Dorchester):*

Property: Mansion or dwelling house, barns, stables, orchards, and garden. Grove (?)d. Moore. (8 acres).
Two acres of meadow in Sopley Mead, one called Withpitt and one called Three Yards.
Half an acre in Dole Mead, near River Avon.
Piece of Arable at Westfield Gate (3 acres).
Westfield Close (3 acres, arable and pasture).
12 acres of arable in North Field.
3 acres at Northfield Gate.
3 acres near Somerfield Barrs.
Half an acre (being a head half) near Derriott Lane.
Half an acre near Ripley Marke.
1 acre near Harper Lane.
3 acres (being a head acre) running from Ripley Marke to John Elliott's Craught.
1 acre abutting the head acre, about 4 acres breadth from the Lanchett.
All of which were late parcel of Sopley Farm and reputed to be late demesne lands of the Manor of Sopley, and late in the tenancy of John and Richard Deane. With fishing rights in the River Avon.

EXCEPTING: Rights to cut timber.
              Leave to keep the manor courts in the mansion house.
              Rights of access through Grove and Moore into Cowleaze.
              Rights to dig soil for repair of hatches & mill ponds at Sopley Mill.
RENT: 20s. per annum, payable at Michaelmas and the Annunciation of St Mary (29th Sept & 25th March).

42: The Squire's Tale

COVENANT: To keep the property in good repair.
To entertain four people for one day at his own cost when the manor court is held.

In 1725, James Willis "of Ringwood, gent", bought both the manor of Sopley, of which Sopley Park was a prominent part, and the advowson of the church from Sir Henry Joseph Tichborne. On his death in 1755 his son John, also of Ringwood, inherited the title of Lord of the Manor and the property. This John of Ringwood died in 1779, having willed the manor to his nephew, John Compton of Minstead. The property passed to his younger brother, James, who had become Vicar of Sopley in 1746 and was squarson of the village until 1770. His son, also called James, was only 16 when his father died, and he was ordained and instituted in 1779. This very long-serving vicar is thought to have rebuilt Sopley House about 1790. He was an enthusiastic sheep farmer and was instrumental in the spreading of Merino sheep farming which became all the rage towards the end of the century. Merino rams were distributed to various people living in the neighbourhood of Sopley, and the Rev Willis appears to have had a big hand in their distribution. Merino sheep were a small short-woolled breed, bred chiefly for their fine wool.

James Willis's son, George Brander Willis, lived for a time in Sopley Park. Then a tenancy agreement dated 21st December 1838 indicates a change of residence. *(The Willis/Bramble Agreement 1838 (ref: D546/5616/13) from the Red House Museum Archive at Dorset County Record Office).* This agreement is quoted now in some detail because of its intrinsic interest in the Sopley story. It relates to:

> *"All those pasture lands or grounds situate lying or being at Sopley aforesaid heretofore thrown together and laid down as a lawn or park and better known by the name or description of Sopley Park, containing an estimated 56 acres."*

The messuage or mansion, in which Mary Willis was residing, was excluded from the agreement, as were the gardens, paths, and passages belonging thereto. Also excepted were all timber, shrubs, and saplings, and the liberty to fell, cut down, grub up, take and carry away the same; also all game and 'rabbitts' with liberty to enter the grounds to hunt and shoot. The tenancy was to start on 23rd December 1838 for one year, and so from year to year. The yearly rent has risen to £168 "of lawful British money". Every acre of land which John Bramble might "plough, dig, or break up or convert to tillage" should carry an extra yearly rental of £30. The tenant also agreed to pay and discharge "all tithes, rates, assessments, and taxes in respect of the said ground except Land Tax, and shall and will at his own expense keep all the hedges, ditches, gates, stiles and fences in a state of good repair". The tenant was not permitted to cut grass on any part of the leased grounds. He was entitled to graze sheep, but no other animals whatsoever; he was allowed to feed turnips, hay or straw to the sheep only in those places where they had been fed in the past. He was not allowed to drive his sheep through the wicket gate near to the dwelling house then occupied by Mr Ireland. A variety of safeguards concerning non-payment of rent, sub-letting, etc. are listed.

In 1843 George Willis sold 81 acres, including Sopley Park House, to William Tice, who had bought some of the land from him as early as 1825. William Tice was the son of William Tice of Ringwood, who died in 1824. William the younger died in 1866. At one time he was in partnership with Martin Kemp-Welch (died 1837), as bankers in Christchurch, under the name of Tice, Welch and Co.

It is interesting to discover documents relating to the claiming of rights in or over the New Forest, as laid down in 14 and 15 Victoria cap. 76, signed by William Tice on 23rd March 1852. In detail the claim was for Common of Pasture for all cattle called Rother Beasts and Horse Beasts, and for Hogs. Also Turbary for the collection of turf, heath and Furze, the right to cut fern and dig marl, and the right to take fuel for every dwelling house or cottage, without number or stint, according to the usage of the Forest.

The listed places on which Tice based his claim of New Forest rights, and which he held the legal estate in fee simple were:

Elliott's Farm – A dwelling house and garden, 3 cottages and land.
Wright's Farm – A dwelling house, 3 cottages and land.
Abbey Farm – A dwelling house, 2 cottages and land.
Willis's – A dwelling house, 3 cottages and land.
Norris's – 2 cottages and land.
4 cottages, garden and land.
House, 2 cottages, garden and land at Ripley.
Cottage and land at Bransgore.
The application cited the existing annual payments to the crown:
        Forest dues – 12s. 6d.
        Fern ticket – 2s. 6d.
        Fern and Fuel ticket – 2s. 6d.
There was also a sum of 6s. 6d. per annum Forest dues paid for the tithing of Sopley and collected by rate on the owners of cottages in the said tithing.

44: The Squire's Tale

As will be seen in the chapter dealing with the Commons, Mr Tice was an active campaigner for the upholding of the rights and privileges of the Freeholders of Sopley. His family were well-known Nonconformists and during William's time at the Park there is evidence of at least one large Temperance fête there.

At this time the estate was comprised chiefly of land formerly owned by families long connected with the locality, e.g. Elliot, Willis, Sabine, Whicher and Wright. Its total acreage was 431.1.20, including Sopley Park House. The Elliot family, who resided in the Homestead (then called Racedalls), is reputed to have lived on the site since the Conquest and the head of the family is recorded in *Domesday* as a huntsman and holder of Ripley, time having corrupted the name of Ulviet to that of Elliot. Many of the family are buried in Sopley Churchyard, the earliest headstone being that of Elizabeth Pears, daughter of John Elliot of Sopley, who died in 1694. The name appears in the church registers from this earliest date – one John Elliot was churchwarden in 1714. Susanne Elliot sold her interest, which she had inherited from Ruth Elliot (widow of John Elliot) to William Tice in 1822.

When William Tice died, the particulars and measurements of the lands and premises in the Manor of Sopley are listed as:

Henry Whicher: Sopley Farm. Mixture of arable, pasture, meadow, 1 wood, 2 withies, 3 homes. Total area 208.2.21.
Robert Paris: Sopley Villa, pasture, meadow, 3 buildings. Total 23.0.14.
Robert Blacklock: Arable, meadow, pasture. Total 8.4.0.
James Moyle: Arable, meadow, pasture, 2 buildings. Total: 32.2.12.
James Wright: Arable, meadow. Total 2.2.24.
J. Wright: Arable, 1 garden, 1 cottage site. Total 2.2.32.
William Tuck: Pasture, meadow. Total 2.1.28.
(?) Parrett: Arable. Total 26.1.30.
Mrs Hawgood: Avon Bank Cottage. 1 house, 2 unspecified entries.
George Reekes: Pasture, arable, 1 home. Total 13.2.12.
John Reekes: Blacksmith, plot next churchyard, hard and smith's shop, 1 other plot. Total 1.2.11.
Representatives of the late William Tice: Meadow, arable, pasture, 7 buildings.
George Ogg: cottage & garden; Mary Pitt: cottage & garden; Mary Gulliver and I. Moyle: two tenements; Joseph Miller: cottage & garden; William Tuck: cottage & garden; Stephen Tuck: cottage & garden; W. Dowden: cottage & garden; T. Kerley: cottage & garden; Button & Linnyton: 3 tenements &

garden; Edward Jones: cottage & garden; John White: cottage & garden; W. Dowden: cottage, garden & stable; W. Summers: cottage & garden; A. Court: cottage & garden; William Poulter: cottage & garden; G. Corbin Jnr.: house, carpenter's shop, yard; T. James: new cottage & garden; H. Butler: 2 tenements & garden; H. & G. Barrow: 2 tenements at Ripley; G. Legg, J. Legg, W. Barnes: 3 tenements at Ripley; Henry Poulter: 2 tenements & garden.

John Kemp-Welch was a London merchant who had acquired the firm of Schweppes in 1834. The origins of his hyphenated family name may be found in an extract from the *London Gazette* dated 16th May 1795:

"The king has been pleased to grant unto Martin Kemp, of Tower Hill, son of Martin Kemp of Poole, Dorset, His Royal Licence and Authority, that he and his issue may take the name of 'Welch', in addition to that of 'Kemp', in compliance with the wish of his maternal Uncle, George Welch, Esq., of the City of London, Banker.

John lived at the Clock House, Clapham Common, and he came to live at Sopley Park and House after his purchase of the property in 1867. On his death in 1885 it was bought for £35,000 by John Kemp-Welch Junior, whose biographical details appear in the chapter on Sopley Worthies.

A description of the estate, drawn up in 1867, reads as follows:

"The Estate, the total area of which is about 720 acres, is freehold with the exception of two or three small pieces held for long terms of years. It is situate in the parishes of Sopley and Christchurch, and is about three miles from Christchurch and six from Ringwood, both with first class railway stations and there is a small station at Herne, one and a half miles distant. There is an excellent family residence close to the village of Sopley, standing in a small timbered park, and surrounded by beautifully shrubbed gardens and pleasure grounds. The residence is approached from the high road by a carriage drive with two very ornamental entrance lodges. It is a very substantial structure, brick and slated and we understand it was considerably added to by the late owner. It is in excellent repair and fitted throughout with pitch pine fittings and the present owner has laid on the electric light throughout. It contains entrance lobby with cloakroom, large dining room, library, drawing room, study, and a very handsomely fitted billiard room, W.C. and lavatory. On the upper floor, approached by front and back staircases, are twelve bed and dressing rooms, bathroom and W.C. The offices comprise kitchen, scullery, servants hall, larders, storerooms. There are spacious cellars and outoffices, and an engine room with fitted engine.

Sopley Park Mansion.
Photograph loaned by Brian Sims.

The stables are removed from the house and are in an enclosed yard, and comprise coach house, stabling for six horses, harness room, coachman's house and turret. There is an excellent walled kitchen garden with conservatory, storehouse, propagating house, vineries and orchard houses.

There is a Home farmstead standing in the park, with two newly-built cottages, yard, cattle sheds, barn, etc. and an ornamental dairy.

There is a small residence known as 'The Elms', brick and slated and situate in the village, containing hall, dining room, drawing room, smoking room, six bedrooms, bathroom, kitchen, scullery, pantry, etc. There is a pretty garden and paddock, in all about four acres, let at sixty pounds a year, and another residence containing two sitting rooms, five bedrooms, and a small stable and garden, let at thirty pounds a year.

A large portion of the village of Sopley belongs to the estate and there are about thirty small holdings, including two village shops, blacksmith's shop, school house cottages and accommodation closer to the village which are let to various tenants and with the above two residences produce a total of £274 a year. In addition there are twelve cottages and two entrance lodges held in hand for the use of the labourers, of a rental value of £60.

The cottages referred to are chiefly brick and tiled and in some cases thatched

Sopley Park Mansion, early twentieth century.
Photograph loaned by Geoffrey Grindle.

and all are in good repair. There is also an excellent farmhouse in the village about to be converted into a double tenement, but worth at least £25 a year, and detatched from it are an excellent set of farm buildings with stable, barn and cattle sheds. The remainder of the estate consists of meadow, pasture and arable lands, with an excellent farmhouse and three sets of farm buildings, most conveniently placed.

The property was, we understand, purchased by the late owner many years ago and he added to it considerably by the purchase of interlying properties from time to time and, wishing to farm it himself, he has had the land on his own hands for many years. The arable land is a rich and productive loam and is chiefly what is known as good sheep and barley land. It is in a very high state of cultivation and we have seldom seen over land more even in quality or in better condition. The present owner who in fact farmed the land previous to his father's death, keeps on an average flock of about a thousand sheep and a hundred head of cattle, including a dairy of forty cows, from which he sends supplies to Bournemouth. The land is well-intersected with roads and there is a good water supply. The meadows are watered by the River Avon flowing through them and are a very useful addition to the farms. The farm buildings are in good order and a carpenter and a bricklayer are kept regularly on the estate. The district is a very

Sopley Park Mansion. The Entrance Hall.
Showing Janus partially obscured by light fitting and some of the winter months.
Photograph loaned by Brian Sims.

49: The Squire's Tale

favourable one for residential purposes and there are a great many residences in the immediate neighbourhood."

When John Kemp-Welch died in 1939 the estate passed to his son Hubert who lived until 1976. His son Ralph was killed in action in the Second World War. Soon afterwards, Sopley Park and House were sold and Hubert Kemp-Welch and his wife went to live at 'The Homestead', formerly 'The Elms'. Sopley Park was in turn a nursing home and two independent schools. The house was demolished in 1988 and with it went a number of treasures, including the French turretted roof and the panelled gentlemen's smoking room. A series of stained glass windows told the story which has become so much part of local folk-lore. In them were depicted the slaying of William Rufus in the New Forest, and the re-shoeing backwards of Sir Walter Tyrell's horse by the blacksmith at Avon. The last window showed the blacksmith lying dead, apparently summarily dispatched by Sir Walter so that his secret could remain intact. In the entrance hall, painted on canvas, were representations of the seasons of the year and the signs of the Zodiac. Pride of place over the fireplace was taken by Janus, holding a babe in one hand and a scythe in the other. Doubtless in the pantries there would have been ample provision of those thick slate slabs so useful for the storage of cheese and butter; some of these remain in place in the lodges.

Sopley Park School opened in 1953; it had as its motto *'cueillez et gardez'* (gather and conserve) and its badge was a squirrel. Sopley Park now contains a number of modern buildings which form the thriving Moorlands Bible College. The old way of life may be seen in the mind's eye only. Take a peep on a Saturday morning; this was pay day, and picture the respectful and regimented gathering of the workers, each ready to doff his cap and step forward to receive his wages for the week.

Sopley Park Mansion. Some of the staff, early 20th century.
Photograph loaned by L. Freeman.

Your Carriage Awaits You. Sopley Park Mansion 1908 (c).
John and Julie Kemp-Welch and Hubert.
Note the Kemp-Welch monogram above the main doorway.
Photograph loaned by Geoffrey Grindle.

51: *The Squire's Tale*

SOPLEY PARK FARM SALE. October 15 1867.

Abstract of items from the machines and implements section together with a note of prices reached at the sale.

£3 3s 0d	A Rocks patent weighing machine and 13 weights.
£12 10s 0d	A capital rick covering, 30ft long, with ropes and pulleys.
8s 0d	A seed sewing machine.
£1 14s 0d	A Pearce's patent corn bruiser.
£1 8s 0d	A Pierce's oil cake crusher.
£1 11s 0d	Gardener's patent turnip cutting machine and trough.
£1 10s 0d	Samuel's patent pulper.
£13 0s 0d	3 horse power thrashing machine – Tasker.
£5 5s 0d	Tasker's horse patent broadcast sowing machine.
£5 0s 0d	Corn drill.
10s 0d	Pair of leaf drags.
17s 0d	Pair of harrows with weys and whippences.
£1 17s 0d	Set of three zigzag iron harrows.
£1 18s 0d	Chain harrow.
£2 0s 0d	Tasker's YD iron plough with skim coulter & whippences.
£1 7s 0d	One-horse turnip hoe.
£2 4s 0d	Bentall's patent three-share scarifier.
£10 10s 0d	Tasker's three-horse 23 in. iron ring-roller.
£7 0s 0d	Tasker's two-horse double cylinder iron roller.
£6 10s 0d	36 in. one-horse park iron roller.
£2 10s 0d	Two-horse land presser.
£1 17s 0d	One-horse iron rake.
£2 4s 0d	Holmes's one-horse patent manure drill.
£3 15s 0d	Water cart & liquid manure pump with gutta perch piping.
£3 5s 0d	Timber nib.
£8 5s 0d	Capital winnowing machine by Baker.
£16 0s 0d	each. Several two or four-horse wagons.
£6 0s 0d	each. Several manure carts.
£4 0s 0d	Capital spring chair.
£1 0s 0d	Invalid's chair.
8s 0d	Cattle tube & chondrometer.
£2 0s 0d	Double barrel gun.

52: The Squire's Tale

Abstract of items from horses and harness.

£18 18s 0d	An excellent brown cart-horse, DUKE.
£1 5s 0d	Set of Thill harness.
£7 7s 0d	Capital bay cart-horse, PRINCE.
£5 10s 0d	Grey cart-horse, PEG.
£5 5s 0d	Capital black cart-horse, SMILER.
£1 1s 0d	each. Several sets of trace harness.
£7 5s 0d	Brown cart-mare, BROWN.
15s 0d	each. Several sets of plough harness.
£3 10s 0d	Carriage harness with covered furniture.

Dairy utensils.

1s 6d	each. 3 brown milk pans & a Sunderland cream pan.
11s 0d	5 circular milk tins.
17s 0d	6 square milk tins.
15s 0d	each. 2 patent butter churns.
11s 0d	A trendle, pair of butter scales, 3 weights, 8 butter prints.
16s 0d	2 tin milk pails & strainer.
14s 0d	Mash tub, funnel, 2 brewing utensils.
8s 0d	4 36 gallon casks.
2s 0d	each. 1 eighteen gallon cask & 1 six gallon cask.

Photograph loaned by Bob Harrison.

The Common Lands of Sopley

Common lands and rights of common were, for hundreds of years, an integral part of the system by which land was cultivated and farmed in England. In the Tithing of Sopley three areas of common land have existed through the centuries. These areas are known as: Jocktrill Common, containing an area approximately 27 acres, predominantly on the eastern bank of the mill stream below Wild Weirs; Vatchers Common, earlier known as Batchers, a long narrow strip of land containing just under two acres, straddling Sopley Brook just north of the forge; and Sopley Common, an area of considerable acreage in the north-western corner of the parish. These areas are certainly not mere relics of a byegone age, for they continue to be the subject of correspondence and the nicer distinctions of law. What are the rights and privileges involved, and who is entitled to receive them? A starting point is provided with a list of all the names of the persons that have 'a Right in Baches' taken from all the old men in the Tithing of Sopley, October 18, 1731.

Benjamin Legg for Coffins Living	1731
Richard Elliott for Georges & John Lean Living	1732
Jonathan Elliott for Fluens & Randels Living	1733
John Elliott for Moyles & Jonathan Elliott for Windefers	1734
Groces Living & John Elliott for Hackmens	1735
Joseph Markins two Livings	1736
John Elliott for his Living at Clapcotts	
Thomas King for two foals	1737
Margaret Kerley John Lean Jas Budden Jonathan Elliott for late Benjamin Elliott being four foals	1738

Almost exactly one hundred years later, a document was prepared by William Tice, Esq. dated June 15 1832, and signed by the inhabitants of Sopley as under:

> "The rights and privileges of the Freeholders of Sopley having been of late years much trespassed upon by persons turning in more cattle to graze than their rights would authorise. Also by persons cutting turf and carrying it away and also by persons cutting the spire before the time allowed by ancient custom. We whose names are undersigned, being Freeholders and desirous of preserving the ancient ways as far as possible and at the same time promoting the benefit of all persons concerned therein do agree to the following proposition

namely that any person occupying a house in the village of Sopley and keeping a horse for the purpose of trade, or a cow, shall by reason of such occupation exercise one right either for such horse or cow but any person having a horse that is not used by him in any profitable employment shall not exercise a right for such horse unless he be the occupier of land sufficient to entitle him under the provisions of this agreement to turn two cows to common. If any householder also be the occupier of one acre of land situated within this village of Sopley he shall by reason of such occupation be permitted to turn one cow to common in addition to the one right granted on behalf of his house and if he occupy three acres of land so situated he shall turn two cows to common as before mentioned. These propositions being an indulgence and not the bestowment of any right on the part of the freeholders who have rights in the common to those who occupy ground for the sustenance of their cattle during the winter season. It is designed on the part of those who have subscribed it that it should be limited to the extent of occupation and privilege which are herein specified. And we furthermore, to protect our rights against all persons who at any time or may cut any spire before the customary time which is fourteen days after Whit Monday in any year. It is further agreed by all whose names are hereunder subscribed, that in no case shall any right be transferred to any person either by sale or gift but if any person having a right or privilege and this agreement shall not occupy or make use of such right or privilege himself, it shall then be considered as forfeited to the use and benefit of those who do exercise their right and to them only."

June 18 1832. W. Tice Esq.; Thos. Blacklock; Thos. Woods; Thos. Wareham; Edmund Budden; Henry Whitaker; Louisa Crouch; Wm. Bowden; Mary Barrow; Rev J Willis; Mary Crouch; James Hogarth; Richard Clapcott; John Bramble Jr.; Richard Corbin; Stephen Hiscock.

A classification of Rights of Common includes rights appendant, rights appurtenant, rights in gross, and rights per cusse de vicinage. In the case of common appendant the right of pasture is limited to "commonable cattle" that is, horses and oxen to plough the land and sheep to manure it. Here there was usually a restriction of numbers. There are no such definite restrictions or limits with common appurtenant; this depends upon the extent of enjoyment proved or upon terms of the grant and so a right might well be restricted to pasturing such animals as hogs, goats and geese, and these in turn may be

55: The Common Lands of Sopley

restricted in numbers. Common in gross may be enjoyed by any animal and usually there is no objection in principle to the existence of pasture without stint, or in other words the right to put on an unlimited number of cattle on the servient tenement. The rights per cusse de vicinage cover a situation where two commons are adjacent and unfenced and the rights of cattle to stray and to feed on each of the two commons.

Account and Minute books exist for the Tithing of Sopley, dating back to 1805. In those days the Tithing man was an unpaid, and sometimes unwilling member of the community, elected to office by Justices of the Peace. His duties included matters of law which, after 1840, were taken over by the parish constable. The earliest entries in the Sopley Tithing book name the Tithing man as Thomas Wood, and between then and 1830 the Tithing men for Sopley included Thomas Bourne, William Ward Wright, Robert Bound, George Barrow, Henry Foster, Edmund Budden, George Rose, John Barrow, James Hogarth and James Woods.

It might be anticipated that the minutes of the regular annual meetings would show a decline in the amount and variety of business as they run from the 19th to the 20th centuries. In fact the opposite is the case. The brief annual accounts occupy most space until the 1890's are reached. These include the annual payment of Forest dues and Court fees, Jury list oath, and a particularily interesting regular entry of expense involved in law day silver. Frequent small amounts were paid to the carpenter and the blacksmith, and digging, fencing, and cleaning tasks all involved routine expenditure. There were also annual references to the sharing of rights and duties. In 1815 a list of persons deemed to be suitable to serve as hayward for the year is given as: John Elliott, Wm. Ward Wright, Robert Bound, Edward Sabine, Richard Clapcott, Thomas Woods; the hayward was an official responsible for the overseeing of the upkeep of hedges, ditches, and fencing.

When the 1890's are reached however the picture becomes a much more assorted one. Sopley Common begins to appear regularly on the agenda. One of the earliest references that has come to light regarding Sopley Common is an "indenture tripartite" made on 30 July 1725 between Sir Henry Joseph Tichborne, John Willis the younger of Ringwood, and Aaron Jeffery(s) of Bransgore – yeoman. For the sum of thirty pounds of "lawfull money of groat" Sir Henry and John Willis sold to Aaron those brick kilns situated upon Sopley Common, and the right to dig, take and cast up turf and so much earth and clay out of the said common, to convert into bricks or tyles. Aaron was enjoined to "level the pits where he had worked". Strangely enough, at the time when the Christchurch – Ringwood railway was being discussed, there is no reference in the Commons Committee minutes of the implications of part of the railway's route being across Sopley Common. From other sources it can be discovered that on Tuesday, 7 February 1860, a special meeting was convened at the Woolpack for those people interested in the Commons' Rights on Sopley and Avon Commons. The object of the meeting was to appoint a committee of Commoners to treat with the promoters of the Ringwood, Christchurch and Bournemouth railway, for compensation to be paid to Commoners for the extinction of their rights in such parts of these common lands as are required and intended to be taken for the purpose of the railway. The Sopley Commoners Committee chosen was Messrs. W. Tice, F. Honeywell, and H. Clapcott; members chosen for the Avon Commoners' Committee were Messrs. W. Tice, T. H. Tuck, and W. Buckland.

Eventually the problem of railway compensation was settled. In 1902 the Christchurch Rural District Council applied to the Sopley Freeholders for sanction to erect a temporary smallpox hospital in case of necessity, on land to the north of the road leading from Herne(!) Station to Herne Bridge. It was resolved that permission be granted on a payment of one pound per annum and an undertaking to repair any damage caused.

A further question of compensation for loss of rights on Sopley Common arose during the Second World War, when in 1941 the Air Ministry requisitioned three acres of land there. By 1955 when the Ministry of Civil Aviation had given notice of their intention to terminate the occupancy of the common, the area involved had risen to approximately ten acres. Eventually in 1963 the work of reinstatement of Sopley Common land had been completed.

Battles over trespass and encroachment, over tipping of rubbish and abuse of commoners' rights were frequent. For a few years there was disagreement between the local squire and the Commons Committee over the boundaries between Jocktrill Common and estate land, including the mill stream. Straying cattle, illicit boating and swimming on and in the millstream, were among the several bones of contention.

Many constructive projects were also pursued, many of them involving the imposition of levies of amounts varying from one shilling to four. In addition to 'wear and tear' repairs, a bridge was built over the spring in Jocktrill, commemorative trees, rhododendrons, and laurels were planted on the commons. In 1951 arrangements were made to fill in the dump at Vatchers with surplus soil from RAF excavations at Ripley. Correspondence took place over the possibility of creating a sports ground for the villagers at Jocktrill – but this was not to be.

A walk round Jocktrill today is a pleasant exercise and affords a peaceful communion with the living past. Jocktrill Shute is the name given to the right of way that leads from the one-way system on the main road down to the

57: The Common Lands of Sopley

meadow–land on the eastern bank of the mill race. This was the way that the cows from Hatch Farm used to make their way to the meadows. It is very much over-grown and a paradise for domestic pets. Until comparatively recently a mud-house stood on the left hand side of the path, going down, where brambles now have free rein, and pig styes abounded on the right.

A stile and a gate afford access to a land of river, stream, spring, meadow, and ditch. The mill-stream was last dredged, with dragline, in 1951, and the waterway was cleared right back to the existing bank. In less than forty years there has been very considerable silting up and in places, between the water and the bank there are now several feet of muddy vegetation, including a quantity of spire which continued to be collected in considerable amounts until very recent times. Spire, or reed stalks, were much sought after for thatching hay and corn ricks, just as the withy beds provided the raw materials for basket-making. This was a considerable cottage industry in Sopley; there is documentary reference to the Withy pitt in Sopley Mead in 1701.

In the years immediately after the end of the Second World War, in addition to dredging the mill-stream, a series of ditches was dug which helped to improve considerably the drainage of this area. Now it is only when the river is in full spate that the strange area of the five islands stands clearly revealed; formerly these islands were almost permanently surrounded by water. The islands form part of the Jocktrill Commons and the slightly lower lands around them form part of the Sopley Estate. No wonder disputes over boundaries and trespass and wandering cattle were so numerous. The five islands can be readily distinguished today, even without the help of the flood waters. Each island has its name. In descending order of size they are called: Big, Drag, King's Hole, Reek's Gaze, and Mint Bed. Big island is so called because of its size. Drag island is the land on to which the horses customarily pulled the debris collected by the drag line. The origin of the name King's Hole has not come to light; the nearby waters were famous for their pike. Reek's Gaze appears to have been named after John Reeks who lived at Chiltley House, overlooking Jocktrill; he also established Reek's Point, a shooting copse close to the main river and alongside Vicarage Point, set in a small area of glebeland. Mint Bed is the smallest island of this former archipelago, named after the profusion of mint growing there. The whole area is rich in gravel and springs; a disused gravel pit exists just east of Drag island.

Here then is an area of land, largely unseen and yet within almost braking distance of the daily passing of literally hundreds of motor vehicles. It is rich in atmosphere and to sit in its midst and contemplate is both refreshing and rewarding. A few yards to the north of Wild Weirs, where the mill-race leaves the river, is the site where the old road to Hurn was bridged across the water.

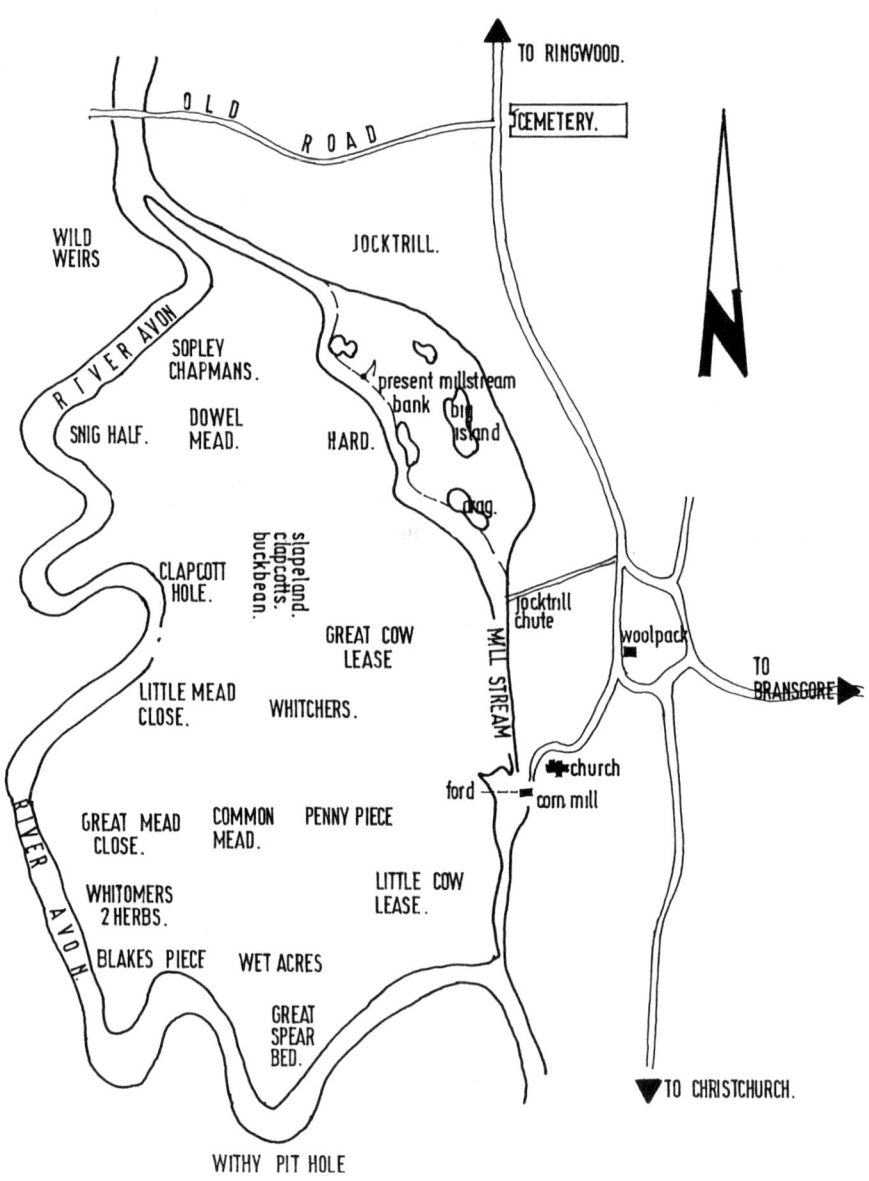

59: The Common Lands of Sopley

To the south of Jocktrill is a heronry, centuries old. Round the bend, to the immediate south of the shute, is the silent mill, which served the local community from the 1940's back to Domesday and beyond. In the imagination can be pictured the journey of a small boat upstream to where a few cows are grazing. The cows are milked while tethered to the fence nearby and the boat returns to its mooring at the shute with its nourishing cargo.

As the shadows lengthen the boat may be seen quietly making its way upstream, with a very young crew intent on the discovery of the nests of coots and moorhens; and in the background the bells of St Michael echo up and down the valley in harmony with the one-time 'mother' church at Christchurch Twyneham.

Wills

Modern research facilities make the study of wills a fascinating occupation. The more detail which is supplied the more the consciousness grows of a sense of privilege, for it is the nature of a sacred privilege to be allowed to contemplate the private thoughts and decisions of those who have lived many generations ago.

Two examples of 17th century wills follow and it will be seen that there is link between them. In each case a photocopy of the original will is followed by a transcription which helps to make clear parts which otherwise might remain obscure.

1630. WILLIAM SANDERS   HUSBANDMAN OF SOPLEY.

(Hampshire Record Office Ref 1630 A82.
Reproduced by permission of the County Archivist.
Transcription by Phillipa White, Assistant Archivist)
(The Sanders family lived in Sopley for many generations).

Jesus.

In the name of God: Amen Anno Domini 1630 And in the 10th of September I William Sanders of the parishe of Soplie in the countie of Southampton husbandman being sicke in bodie but hole in mind and in perfect memorie doe macke my will and Testament in manner and forme folowinge first I bequeth my soule to allmightie god my macker and onlye sauviour & my bodye to be bured in the Churche yeard of my parishe of Soplie: In primis I give to John Sanders my sonne £3 one year after my deces I give to Thomas Sander my sonne 20s to be payd in one yeare afte my deces Item I give to Jane Sanders my daughter 20s to be payd in one yeare after my deces Item I give to Christine Sanders my daughter the monie which ys in the handes of Jeames Markett which is the sume of fiftie three shellinges fower pence Item I give to Marye Sanders my daughter the monie which ys in the handes of Thomas Burke scrivener (?) the sum of fourtie shillinges: Item I give to Richard Sheephard my daughters sonne one heffer bullock of a year old: Item I give to John Sanders my sonne one pece of newe clothe and a payr of hose & shewes & one peticott: Item I give to Thomas Sanders my sonne all the rest of my weringe parell Item I give to William Sanders my brothers sonne 6d: all the rest of my goodes movable & unmovable to Anstes Sanders my wiffe whome I macke my whole executor my funerall & debites discharged I cale to record this to be my last will & Testament also I request my beloved in Christe John Sanders and John Brixse to be my oversears to see my will fulfiled & kept & they to have for ther paines tackinge therein 4d appec the wettnes to this will ys John Davie John Brixse with others

John Brixse   his marke   John Davye   his marke

Administration granted to Anastar Sanders, widow by direction of Master marston, Vicar of Cristchurch Master hilliard, vicar of Sopley Bondsman John Sanders of Sopley, yeoman.

An Inventory of all the goodes & Cattell of Willm Sanders late deceased praised the xxiiijth of September by Richard Sanders, Mathewe Cobbett wth others Ao Di 1630

Imprimis his wearinge apparell	xxs
It ij bead stedes j boulster ij payre of blankets ij Coverledes iij payer of sheetes ij pillowes	xxxijs
It j Cubbord	xiijs iiijd
It fower Coffers & one Chest	[illegible]
It one table bord one form wth other bordes	xs
Shelves & stooles	iijs
It two firkinges one kneadell ij one tubbes two boules & one pouderinge tubbe	vjs viijd
It one brass panne iij brasse kettels one brasse potte & j brass skilliat	xxxs
It ij platers iij poringers ij sawcers ij saltes j Candlestickes wth dishes & spoones	vjs
It ij boules j lanthorne one fryinge panne one payre of sheres iij payre of Cottrell ij pair of pott hangers ~~[illegible]~~ j bottle	vs vjd
It some iij wheat ayles ij spades ij j axe [illegible] j shovell j sithe iiij rakes forkes one [illegible] j hammer	viijs
It one ij woollen wheles j linnen wheele wth other tooles	iijs iiijd
It other [illegible] j baskett j sive j [illegible] & wash cardes	iijs viijd
It ~~xiij~~ poundes of course wooll	[illegible]
It butter & cheese & cullenders	[illegible]
It iij kine one steare two heifers	[illegible]
It Rye in the barne	[illegible]
It barlye & oates in the barne	[illegible] iiijd
It wheat in the barne ~~& one bushell [illegible]~~ j bushell of barley & one bushell of wheat at John Dagges j peck of rye & j peck of mault	xvjs
It haye & strawe	xs
It fyve swine hogges	[illegible]
It the hempe wth flagges in garden	js
It one peck of Carrotes	js iiijd
It j hide & j locke	viijd
It in the handes of Andrewe Bates	xxs
It in the handes of John Pecke of Berlington	xxxs
It in the handes of Thomas Andrewe	js
It one Cradle	[illegible]

Som total [illegible]li vs iiijd

An invitory of all the goodes and cattelles of William Sanders late decsed praised the 18th of September by Richard Sanders, Marttine Sebutt with others Anno Domini 1630.

In primis his wearinge parrell	20s	
Item 2 bead stedes, 2 boulster, 2 payer of blanketes, 2 courledes, 3 payer of shetes, 3 pellowes	32s	
Item 1 Cubberd	6s	8d
Item fower Coffers & one Chest	10s	
Item one Table bord, one form with oulde bordes, shelf and stoles	2s	
Item twoe virkings, one treadell, 2 tubbe, twoe coules & one poudringe vessell	6s	8d
Item one bras panne, 4 bras ketteles one brase pootte & 1 brase skelliat	30s	
Item 2 platers, 3 potingers, 2 sassers, 2 saltes, 1 candlestickes with diches & spones	6s	
Item 3 boules, 1 lantren, one fring panne, one payer of whers, 3 (?2) payer of Cottrell, 2 payer of poott hangers & 1 brotche	2s	6d
Item 1 howe, 3 beat axes, 2 spades, 1 axe, 1 hatchat, 1 shovell, 1 sithe, 4 repe hockes, one hetchell, 1 hammer	7s	
Item 2 woottornes, 1 lintorne with seves & other earth vesselles, 1 peck, 1 baskett, 1 renge, 1 serche 6 woole cardes	4s	
Item 12 poundes of Corse woole	3s	4d
Item butter & cheese culliners	7s	
Item 3 Kine, one steare, twoe heffers	£7 10s	
Item Rye in the barne	30s	
Item barlye & ottes in the barnes	30s	4d
Item wheat in the barne & 1 bushell of barlye & one bushell of wheat at John Tagges, 1 pecke of Rye & 1 pecke of meale	6s	
Item haye & soyle	10s	
Item six swine hogges	27s	
Item the himpe with lagges in gardine	1s	
Item one pocke of Turfes	1s	4d
Item 1 hene & 1 Cocke		8d
Item in the handes of Andrew Bathe	20s	
Item in the handes of John Veche of Bockington	40s	
Item in the handes of Thomas Newen	1s	
Item one Cradell	1s	4d

Sum total £24 5s 4d.

In the name of god Amen I Mari Dorrely of Riply
in the parish of Ripply being sick in bodi but whol
in mind doo make this my last will & testement in
maner and forme as followeth: forst I bequeth my
Soul unto Allmiti god my only Saviour and Redemar
and my bodi to bee buried in the Church yard of Ripply

In primus i giue too the poore ——————— 2 — 0 — 0
Itm i giue too Lazarus warum ——————— 10 — 0 — 0
Itm i goue too Katurn Goben ——————— 0 — 2 — 6
Itm i goue too James Goben ——————— 5 — 0 — 0
Itm i goue too Elisobet Goben ——————— 5 — 0 — 0
Itm i geue too Alis framtun ——————— 4 — 0 — 0
Itm i goue too edward Lorkars dafter — 4 — 0 — 0
Itm i goue too Thomas Bounds Children — 2 — 0 — 0
Itm i goue too Thomas Bound ——————— 0 — 5 — 0
Itm i goue too toone da ——————— 0 — 10 — 0
Itm i geue too John da ——————— 0 — 5 — 0
Itm i goue too Thomas Rorkly ——————— 0 — 5 — 0
Itm i getue too Gobol Bats on Goot ——— 0 — 10 — 0
Itm i goue to Thomas Mosse & henri Mosse — 0 — 10 — 0
Itm i goue to mari Sanders Annes Mathear — 10 — 0

All the rest of my goods I goue too John
Sanders mous abel and Sumous abel and
he too bee my wholl executer

In the presentes of Thomas Bound
Rizard Sanders & Mari Sanders

the 13 of november 1647

THE WILL OF MARI ROWCKLY OF RIPLEY IN THE PARISH OF SOPLEY

*(Hampshire Record Office Ref 1648 A73.
Reproduced by permission of the County Archivist;
transcription by Frances Younsen, Assistant Archivist)*

In the name of god Amen I Mari Rowckly of Ripley in the parish of Sopley beeing sick in bodi but whol in mind doo mack this my last will & testement in manar and forme as followeth ferest I bequeth my Soul unto Allmiti god my only Saviour and Redemar and my bodi to bee bured in the Church yard of Soply

In primus i geeve too the poore	£2	0s 0d
Itu (m) i geeve too Laranes Warum	£10	0s 0d
Itu (m) i geeve too Caturne Goven		2s 6d
Itu (m) i geeve too James Goven	£5	0s 0d
Itu (m) i geeve too Elesebeth Goven	£5	0s 0d
Itu (m) i geeve too Ales Framtun	£4	0s 0d
Itu (m) i geeve too Edward Leckars dafter	£4	0s 0d
Itu (m) i geeve too Thas Boundes cheldren	£2	0s 0d
Itu (m) i geeve too Thomas Bound		5s 0d
Itu (m) i geeve too goone da		10s 0d
Itu (m) i geeve too John da		5s 0d
Itu (m) i geeve too Thomas Rockly		5s 0d
Itu (m) i geeve too Sebel Bath on Coot		10s 0d
Itu (m) i geeve too Thomas Mest & Henri Mest		10s 0d
Itu (m) i geeve too Mari Croker & Annes Wettear		10s 0d

All the rest of my goodes I geeve too John Sanders movabel and unmovabel and he to be my wholl execketer
in the presentes of Thomas Bound Richard Sandars & Mari Sandars
the 13 of november 1647

endorsed on back: Itum i geeve to Gras Bound 10s.

66: Wills

Glossary of words found in William Sanders' inventory:

courledes	probably coverlets (not found in any glossaries).
virkinges	firkins or small casks for liquids, fish, butter, etc., originally holding a quarter of a barrel.
coule	cowl or a tub, cask or vat especially one with two ears borne by two men on a cowl staff.
poudringe tub	powdering tub or tub in which the flesh of animals was powdered or salted or pickled.
skelliat	skillet or cooking utensil of brass, copper or other metal with a 3'-4' long handle used for boiling liquids, stewing meat, etc.
potinger	pottinger or a vessel made of metal, earthenware or wood for holding soup, broth, etc.; a small basin.
sasser	saucer
salte	may be a salve or a coverlet.
cottrell	cotterel or a trammel, crane or bar to hang a pot over the fire.
brotche	could be a broach or spike on which to stick a candle, or a pointed rod of wood or iron or a chisel or a spit.
repe hockes	reap hooks or short handled hooks without teeth and a bent blade used to cut a handful at a time.
hetchell	implement for heckling hemp, i.e. combing the coarse fibres from the fine.
peck	two gallon container for dry goods.
renge	a ring or range, a sieve or container.
serche	a search or fine hair sieve.
culliners	probably colanders.
kine	cattle.
soyle	probably soil, but could be a sullow or plough.
lagges	lags or the staves or laths forming the covering of a barrel or cylinder.
pocke	peck (as above).

Poverty

Catastrophic events such as the Black Death in the 14th century and the Plague of London in 1665 used to be items in a long list of historical dates which pupils were required to memorise for examination purposes. Too often too many children never had an opportunity to sit for an examination because they were victims of a scourge which prevailed for centuries and will never altogether go away – the scourge of poverty. Legislation to cope with the problem has been a permanent feature of the statute books for centuries. A study of local records reveals a story that is sad and often gruesome: beggars on the road, the burying of paupers with no known name, regulations concerning when such burials could take place, disease and crime. It was entirely a local responsibility to look after the poor, the aged and the infirm, and the awful weight of this responsibility fell very largely on the shoulders of churchwardens and overseers.

The office of the Overseer of the Poor dates from the great Elizabethan Poor Law of 1601, which was an attempt to draw together under one heading a host of previous acts and regulations. It allowed for the collection of compulsory parochial rates which were raised and managed by overseers. Accounts were ordered to be presented annually to two justices, and the appointment of overseer was to be an annual one, made by magistrates on vestry nomination.

Assistant overseers for the Parish of Sopley in the early 1830s were Robert Blacklock for Sopley, James Sabine for Avon, and Stephen Groves for Ripley and Shirley. Robert Blacklock's duties, at a salary of £30 per annum, were listed as follows:

> *"He shall take upon him the entire charge of the workhouse of the said parish and the superintendence of the poor therein, as to their clothing, diet, and employment. He shall pay the poor in the whole parish in such measure as the Select Vestry shall from time to time order and direct. He shall find work for the unemployed labourers applying for relief and superintend and pay them for their labours. He shall keep a list of all persons employed by the parish in order to supply any application that may be made for labours.*
>
> *He shall attend the Select Vestry at all their meetings and make a report of all his proceedings during the time intervening from meeting to meeting. He shaal conform to, observe, and execute all such orders and directions as he shall from time to time receive from the Select Vestry as to the time and manner of paying the poor and all other matters and things which shall be given to him relative to the*

> *aforesaid objects or any other circumstances which may occur. He shall at the aforesaid meetings of the Select Vestry regularly account for all monies received by him from the overseers and for the earnings of the poor or in any other way or manner and also for the disbursements which he shall have made on account of the said parish. He shall attend Magistrates, and make applications to them for the removal of paupers and or any other parish business as effectually as the Overseers might or could do. He is to be allowed his reasonable travelling expenses when he shall be required to go out of the parish on parish business."*

Events in France towards the close of the 18th century made a tremendous impact in this country in all walks of life, and it is not altogether surprising to learn that workhouses here were frequently referred to as *Bastilles*. The plight of the unemployed and of paupers has evoked a variety of response. A common view among the 'better off' in the England of the early 19th century was that poverty stemmed from bad and weak character rather than misfortune: similar views were expressed in the England of the 1970s and early 1980s.

A poor house for the Parish of Sopley had been established at Avon in the mid-18th century, at a time when Edward Sabine and Francis Pope were Sopley churchwardens. An examination of expenses relating to this house for the year 1833-34 may help an appreciation of the measure of work and responsibility involved: where several entries have been made under the same heading, e.g. supply of faggots, an average cost is attached: wheat (£6 10s 0d per sack); faggots (3s a hundred); barley (£1 10s); butter (10d per lb); cheese (2½d); pigs (£3); salt fish (112 lb for £1 3s 6d); groceries (widely varying); potatoes (15 sacks for £3 15s); pease (£1 8s per sack); medicine (16s 6d); malt (£2 5s); shaving of the poor (3s per quarter); shoes (varying amounts); clothing (varying amounts); yarn (3lb for 7s 6d); annual rental (£12); carriage of coals (14s); turf (£1 10s per load); repair of fencing (£3 12s); coffins (14s each); funeral expenses (4s 6d); master's yearly salary (£15); master's expenses (4s 10d).

Robert Blacklock's accounts show vividly the extent and variety of his tasks. In 1832 thirteen monthly payments to the poor are made, at roughly 6s a head; regular weekly payments to eleven different families of amounts ranging from 2-3 shillings are recorded. A long list of miscellaneous items includes: annual surgeon's payment to Mr Quartly for attendance on the poor, assistance to persons on the road, carriage of loads of turf, horse hire expenses of journeys to Milford and Lymington, making out of jury lists and

69: Poverty

lunatic lists, returns to Parliament, printing bill, child's coffin. His total expenditure in Sopley for the year 1832-33 was £209 8s 8d and his total receipts £217 6s. It is tempting to speculate on the significance of one entry in the Tithing book for 1833: Expenses at the Woolpack 1s 7p!

Some insight into the kind of labouring tasks assembled for the poor is obtained from the accounts of the first half of 1835. A workforce of 22 men was employed in making a bank on the common at Avon, to enclose ten acres of land, and the breaking up of six acres. The men were paid by the lugg, proportionate to the distance involved. A long lugg was paid 1s and a short one 3 pence. Payment for the labour involved in breaking up the common was approximately one shilling per day.

Here are the details of a Bill of Fare for Sopley Work House, sanctioned by the Committee of that house to be enforced from March 25 1825 until March 25 1826:

	BREAKFAST	**DINNER**	**SUPPER**
Mon.	Broth	Rice	Bread & cheese
Tues.	Broth	Beef soup	Bread & cheese
Wed.	Broth	Oatmeal broth	Bread & cheese
Thurs.	Broth	Bread & cheese	Bread & cheese
Fri.	Broth	Pea soup & pork	Bread & cheese
Sat.	Broth	Pease broth	Bread & cheese
Sun.	Bread & cheese	Pork & veg.	Bread & cheese

(From the Red House Museum Archive in the Dorset Record Office. Ref D546/7728).

From 1835 Sopley came within the Union of Christchurch and entries in the accounts for that year tell of the taking down and packing up of bedsteads at the Workhouse. One of the last entries records receipts from the Guardians of the Union at Christchurch of £13 7s 2d and £15 19s 7d, being the value of the provisions and furniture sent into the Poorhouse at Christchurch with the paupers.

It can only be hoped that Robert Blacklock was a willing horse, for following the Highways Act of 1835, in the following year he was appointed Surveyor of the Highways with a salary of £30 a year.

Population

An investigation of population statistics for the village of Sopley carries an inherent complication, in that quoted figures are often those for the parish as a whole. Thus there must be an awareness that a quoted Sopley total will include, not only Sopley tithing, but the tithings of Avon, Ripley and Shirley as well. Later statistics include an ever-multiplying Bransgore, and a figure for Hurn is quoted for 1931.

There seems little doubt that throughout the centuries the whole area has been sparsely populated, in common with very considerable acreages in Hampshire. At the time of *Domesday* the total for the whole of the parish of Sopley might well have been considerably below three figures. Through medieval times there seems likely to have been a gradual increase, unaffected in the long term by fluctuations attendant upon the Black Death and other periods of plague.

The details of regular counts are available for inspection from 1801 onwards, and the census for 1851 affords systematic details, not only of age, but occupations, housing, and places of birth. Indeed, from the beginning of the 19th century, the same names occur in a wide variety of documentation, so that personalities begin to emerge and the story assumes a flesh and blood aspect that is inevitably more and more absent as the journey goes backwards in time.

Between 1841 and 1931 relative tithing populations in the parish can be discerned from the following figures:

1841: **Sopley: 325; remaining tithings: 614.** At this time Sopley had the largest population.

1851: **Sopley: 199; remaining tithings: 697.** In ten years Sopley's numbers have dwindled dramatically and the tithing has been overtaken by both Avon and Ripley. Bransgore (113) is included for the first time.

1871: **Sopley: 160; remaining tithings: 660.** Bransgore figures have increased to 128, Shirley having been overtaken. Further decline at Sopley.

1931: **Sopley: 159; remaining tithings: 737.** Remaining tithings figure includes Hurn (65) for the first time. The Sopley figure is one below the 1871 figure.

Where was Number 200?
A more detailed analysis of Sopley's 1851 census.

A total of 199 persons are listed as living in the village. A prominent (and possibly the only) missing name which would have brought the figure to 200 is that of the Vicar, Rev. J.P. Hammond.

The 199 are shown as living in 43 houses, with three uninhabited (c.f. 41 houses in 1931). Surnames recorded, in alphabetical order, are: Bacon, Barrow, Bennett, Brenton, Budden, Button, Clapcott, Collins, Conway, Corbin, Curtis, Dowden, Earley, Hammond, Harfield, Hindle, Hiscock, Hogarth, Honeyseed, Horlock, Hosking, Jones, Joy, Kearley, Lawford, Lymington, Lyne, Moyle, New, Paris, Parsons, Pitt, Preston, Scrivener, Shave, Stride, Tice, Tizard, Tuck, Vivian, Wareham, Warland, Wheeler.

Listed occupations: 'At home' includes wives (unless otherwise listed) and children too young to attend school. At home: 68; At school: 44; House servants: 18; Labourers: 9; Farm labourers: 7; Gardeners: 4; Wheelwrights: 3; Labourer's assistants: 3; Visitors: 3; Land proprietors: 3; Carpenters: 3; Dressmakers: 3; Apprentices: 2; Housekeepers: 2; Grocers: 2; Farmers: 2; Laundresses: 2; Schoolmistresses: 2; Smith & Inn-keeper: 1; Veterinary surgeon: 1; Cordwainer: 1; Cordwainer's mate: 1; Parish clerk & Schoolmaster: 1; Schoolmaster: 1: Housemistress: 1; Wagoner: 1; Carrier's boy: 1; Mill labourer: 1; Merchant's clerk: 1; Retired carpenter: 1; Accountant: 1; Policeman: 1; Nurse: 1; Glovemaker: 1; Dairyman: 1; Farm holder: 1; Errand boy: 1.

Five of this list were receiving Parish Relief. The occupations list for 1988 would no doubt make an interesting comparison.

Commutation of Tithes

The early years of the 19th century were to see great and lasting changes in the agricultural scene. Reform permeated the discussion chambers at Westminster. On 25th May 1836 the urgent attention of Parliament was again drawn to the subject of agricultural distress in the country, this time by the Marquis of Chandos. He referred to the heavy burdens carried by farmers in the maintenance of prisoners in gaol, the building and repairing of county bridges, the compulsory labour on the highways. It was felt by many that these burdens should be carried by the general taxation of the country and that the duty on widows in farm houses and on horses used in husbandry should be taken off entirely.

It was inevitable that against the background of the Industrial Revolution and the growing power and influence of Nonconformity in the land, tithes should come under the political microscope. From ancient times it had been an obligation of all parishioners to maintain their parish priest from the fruits of the earth in his parish. The great tithe barn was the centre of the scene of this support in kind. Great Tithe, made up of corn, hay and wood, was payable to a Rector. A Vicar, often in addition to a meagre cash stipend, received small tithes on everything else, especially wool and the annual increase of farm stock.

In 1836 Lord John Russell brought before the House of Commons the complicated ministerial plan for the commutation of tithes throughout England. The core of the plan was to set up an organisation by which agreements could be reached between specially appointed commissioners and interested parties over the change-over of tithe obligation from payments in kind to fixed payments. The intended rent charge was to consist of a sum as would, if divided into three equal parts, purchase the same quantity of wheat, barley and oats as tithe produced in 1836. This was an attempt to guard against unfairness to either side resulting from fluctuations in money values or grain prices. Averages were to be worked out over a 10-15 year period. The Tithe Act of 1918 (8 & 9 Geo V c 54) substituted 15 years for the previous 10 year periods and another Tithe Act of 1935-36 (26 Geo V & Ed VIII c 43) made provision for the extinction of tithe rent charges.

A study of the agreements reached in the Parish of Sopley affords a wealth of information relating to families and properties in the mid 19th century. The Tithe Commissioners were named as William Blamire and Richard Jones, the Valuer was Charles Gearing of Kilmiston, and the map of the area was designed by G.H. Whalley, an Assistant Tithe Commissioner. The agreement was dated 18th June 1839 and the parties to the agreement were listed as:

73: Commutation of Tithes

1). Several owners of land within the parish, with an interest of not less than two-thirds of the land subject to tithe.
2). Rev. John Parish Hammond, Clerk, Vicar of the said parish and owner of the Vicarial or Small Tithes thereof.
3). William Wyndham of Dinton, in the County of Wilts, Esquire, Impropriate Rector and owner of the Tithes of Corn and Grain.

In the legal language of the day the agreement proceeds to declare that

"the annual sum of £330 10s by way of rent charge shall be payable and paid to the said John Parish Hammond and his successors instead of all the Vicarial or Small tithes, including Tithe of Glebe, the rent charge in lieu of which it is hereby agreed shall be fixed at the sum of ten shillings in respect of the Vicarial or Small tithes of all the Glebe lands of the said Parish and which item it is hereby agreed shall be apportioned exclusively upon the said Glebe lands, and instead of all Moduses and Compositions real and prescriptive Easter offerings and customary payments payable to the Vicar in respect of all the lands in the said Parish or the produce thereof."

A Modus Decimandi – generally called Modus – could be in the form of money, or as an example, an agreement to take so many hens in lieu of tithe eggs. Such an arrangement was usually held to be legal.

A very similar commentary accompanies the announcement that the annual sum of £550 by way of rent charge be made to William Wyndham, his heirs and assigns, instead of all the Tithes of Corn and Grain of all the lands of the said Parish subject to Tithes. For William Wyndham, the Rent charge in lieu of Tithe of Glebe, is fixed at the sum of Two Pounds.

There follows a schedule to the Articles of Agreement containing a statement of all the particulars required by Act of Parliament:

"The Parish of Sopley contains by estimation: 4,400 acres.
The whole quantity of land subject to payment of
    any kind of Tithes (excl. of Commons):   3,000 acres.
Land subject to Tithe cultivated as Arable: 1,860 acres.
Land subject to Tithe, Meadow or Pasture: 760 acres.
Small tenements, Gardens, Yards, Buildings etc.   150 acres.
Land cultivated as Woodland & Plantation: 230 acres.
Common Land within the Parish: 1,400 acres.

74: Commutation of Tithes

The pasture lands (that is Cowleaze land, fed with cows and never mown) is subject to a modus of 2d for a cow, 2†6 in lieu of a calf or colt, gardens pay 2d each. Bees, faggots, eggs, cocks, hens, geese and ducks pay no tithe.

For the woodlands, two or three pollards or decayed trees have been annually assigned to the Vicar in lieu of Tithes, worth about 10 shillings or twelve shillings a year.

The Commons and Wastelands, mostly covered with Heath and Furze, subject to Common rights of turning out cattle and cutting Turf and furze, for firing, pay no Tithe.

The Glebe lands of the said Parish which, if not in the hands of the owner, would be subject to Tithe, amount by estimation to 40 acres."

The Agreement concludes with the declaration:

"Now I, Charles Gearing of Kilmiston in the County of Hants, having been duly appointed valuer to apportion the total sum agreed to be paid by way of Rent Charge in lieu of Tithes amongst the several lands of the Parish of Sopley, do hereby apportion the Rent Charge as follows:
Gross Rent Charge, payable to the Tithe owners in lieu of Tithes for the Parish of Sopley in the County of Hants: £882 10s 0d.
Value in Imperial Bushels and Decimal parts of an Imperial bushel of wheat, barley, oats:
Wheat 7s 0¼d per bushel.   837.98220 bushels.
Barley 3s 11½d per bushel.   1486.31580 bushels.
Oats   2s 9d   per bushel.   2139.39394 bushels.

A few facts by way of comparison with some of the figures given above are supplied by a record that in 1340 a jury of the Parish of Sopley, consisting of John Le Taweyre, William Luwyne, Robert Anneys, and Robert Murding, assessed the Rectorial Tithes of Sopley at £9 2s 2d. There was a parsonage house & rents worth 13s 4d. The Vicarial Tithes, Oblations and Mortuaries they assessed at 44s 8d.

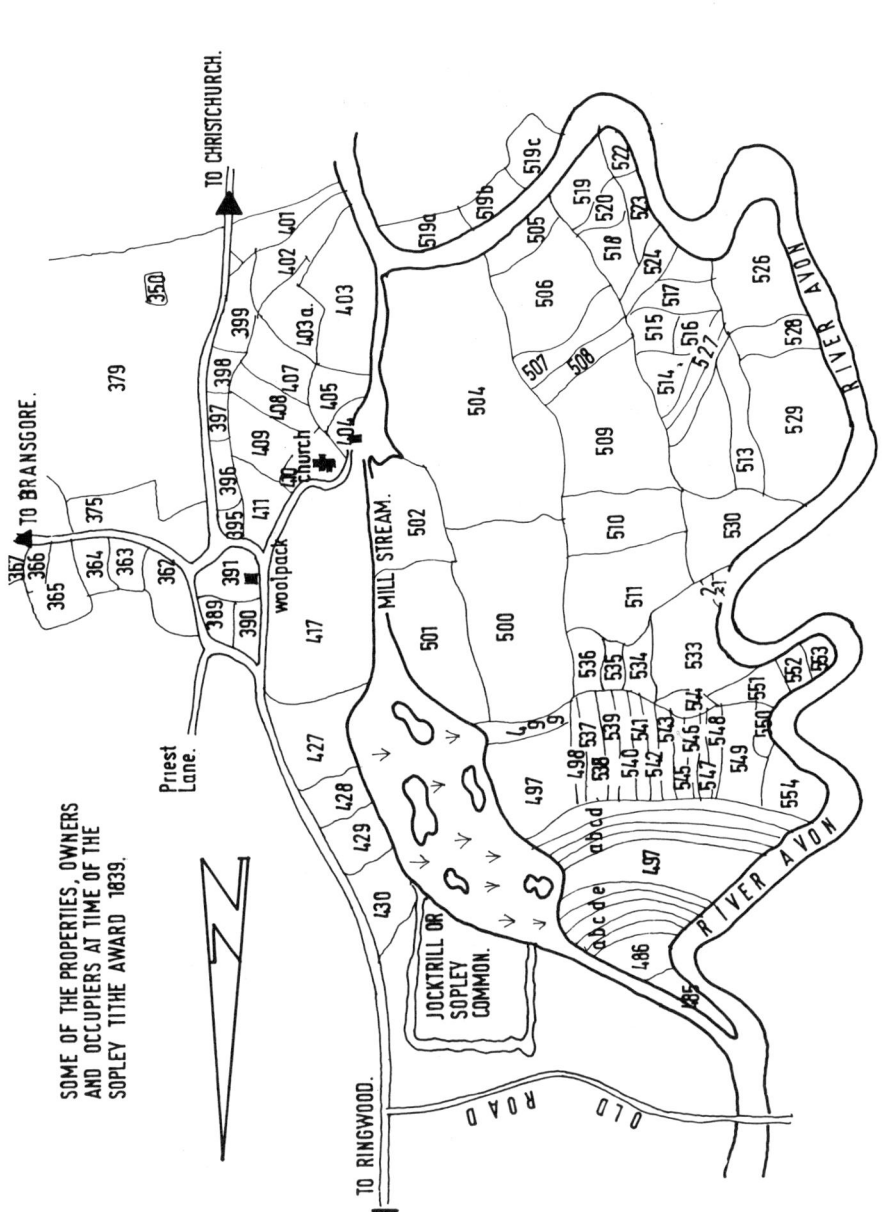

76: Commutation of Tithes

A list of some of the properties, owners and occupiers at the time of the Sopley Tithe Award 1839 (see map).

Map No.	Owner.	Occupier.	Description.
362	W. Tice.		House, garden, premises.
363	Rev. Hammond.	Rev. Veitch.	Vicarage.
364	Rev. Hammond.		Glebe (pasture).
365	Rev. Hammond.		Glebe (pasture).
366	W. Tice.	Jas. Moyle.	Deans.
367	W. Tice.	Jas. Moyle.	Deans.
375.	E. Clapcott.	W. Dowden.	Arable.
379	G.B. Willis.	Self.	Park.
380	G.B. Willis.	Self.	Mansion House.
389	Mrs Martin.	J. Bramble	Plot.
390	Mrs Martin.	J. Bramble.	Plot.
391	J. Pierman.	W. Shave.	Woolpack.
395	W. Tice.	W. Dowden.	Stable, etc.
396	J. Sabine	E. Sabine.	
397	G.B. Willis.		Meadow.
398	E. Budden.	J. Wareham.	Cowleaze.
399	E. Budden.	J. Wareham.	
400	W. Tice.	D. Summers.	Cottage & Garden.
401	G.B. Willis		Cowleaze.
402	E. Budden.	J. Wareham.	Meadow.
403	G. Aldridge.		
404	G. Aldridge.	W. Stride.	
405	G. Aldridge.		Plot.
406	G. Aldridge.		Yard.
407	E. Budden.	J. Wareham.	
408	T. Wareham.	J. Barrow.	Plot adj. churchyard.
409	?	C. Harrison.	
410	Charity School.	R. Keen.	House & Garden.
411	G.B. Willis.	J. Sammers.	Cottage & Garden.
417	W. Tice.	J. Bramble.	Quamp (pasture).
427	E. Budden.	J. Wareham.	
428	Mrs Martin.	J. Bramble.	Barber's Plot (arable).
429	E. Budden.	J. Wareham.	Avon Lane Close (arable).
430	W. Tice.	Jas. Moyle.	Jocktrel (arable).
495	G. Aldridge.		Meadow.

77: Commutation of Tithes

496	G. Aldridge.		Sopley Sharphams.
497	G. Aldridge.		Sopley Sharphams.
497a	G. Aldridge.		Sopley Sharphams.
498	Mary Whitcher.	Herself.	
499	Cath. Weakly.	Herself.	
500	W. Tice.	J. Bramble.	Great Cowleaze (pasture).
501	W. Tice.	J. Bramble.	Millpond.
502	W. Tice.	J. Bramble.	Leggs Mead (meadow).
503	G. Aldridge.	Himself.	Mill, house, premises.
505	W. Tice.	J. Bramble.	Withy Bed.
506	W. Tice.	J. Bramble.	Meadow.
507	W. Tice.	J. Bramble.	Wet 7 Acres (meadow).
508	W. Tice.	J. Bramble.	Roadway.
509	G.B. Willis.	Himself.	Penny's Piece.
510	W. Tice.	Jas. Moyle.	
511	John Sabine.	Edw. Sabine.	Meadow.
513	Mrs S. Woods.	R. Blacklock.	Common Mead.
514a	Eliz. Clapcott.	W. Dowden.	Common Mead.
514b	G.B. Willis.	Himself.	Common Mead.
515	J. Sabine.	E. Sabine.	Home Close.
516	Mrs Martin.	J. Bramble.	Martin's Acre.
517	W. Tice.	J. Bramble.	Isaac's Acre.
518	W. Tice.	J. Bramble.	Wet 4 Acres.
519	G. Aldridge.	W. White.	Meadow.
519a	G. Aldridge.	J. Taylor.	Meadow.
519b	G. Aldridge.	J. Meadus.	Meadow.
519c	G. Aldridge.	H. Barrett.	Plot.
520	W. Tice.	J. Bramble.	Wet Acre in Spear Bed.
521	W. Tice.	J. Bramble.	Double Ditch.
522	W. Tice.	J. Bramble.	Little Spear Bed.
523	W. Tice.	J. Bramble.	Dudmore Mead.
524	W. Tice.	J. Bramble.	Roadway.
526	Mrs Martin.	J. Bramble.	Blake Piece.
528	W. Tice.	J. Bramble.	Whitcher's Acre.
529	W. Tice.	J. Bramble.	Great Mead Close.
530	W. Tice.	Jas. Moyle.	Little Mead Close.
531	Mary Whitcher.	Herself.	Odds.
532	Rev Hammond.		Mead.
533	Eliz. Clapcott.	W. Dowden.	Clapcott's Meadow.
534	W. Tice.	Ben. Tuck.	Slape Lane Mead.

78: Commutation of Tithes

535	Eliz. Clapcott.	W. Dowden.	Meadow.
536	W. Tice.	Ben. Tuck.	Slape Lane Mead.
537	W. Tice	Jas. Hogarth.	In Dowle Mead.
538	W. Tice.	Jas. Bramble.	Dowle Mead.
539	Mrs Martin.	Jas. Bramble.	Dowle Mead.
540	Sir H. Fane.	W. Walden.	In Dowle Mead.
541	Sir H. Fane.	S. Grove.	In Dowle Mead.
542	Richard Wills.	Jo. Buckland.	Dowle Mead.
543	Sir H. Fane.	S. Grove.	In Dowle Mead.
544	Rev Hammond	G.B. Willis.	Meadow.
545	W. Tice.	J. Bramble.	Dowle Mead.
546	Mrs Martin.	J. Bramble.	Dowle Mead.
547	Mary Whitcher.	Herself.	Dowle Mead.
548	W. Tice.	Jas. Hogarth.	Dowle Mead.
549	Mrs Martin.	J. Bramble.	Snig Half (meadow).
550	G.B. Willis.	Himself.	Dowle Mead.
551	G.B. Willis.	Himself.	Dowle Mead.
552	Mary Whitcher.	Herself.	Meadow.
553	Rev Hammond.	G.B. Willis.	Dowle Mead.
554	Mary Whitcher.	Herself.	Dowle Mead.

Roads and Traffic

Queen Mary 1 reigned for a brief five years and if that short time is commonly associated with anything at all, it is almost exclusively with the burning of Protestant heretics. Midway through her reign however, in 1555, parishes were made responsible for the upkeep of their own roads. Local surveyors were required to be appointed by the parish churchwardens and these surveyors were required to supervise the parishioners while working on the roads for an obligatory four days a year. In 1563 the number of compulsory days' work was increased to six and surveyors were granted additional powers to bolster the execution of their duties. Further amendments to the Act were made in 1575 and 1576 and it was made permanent in the year before the Armada came, in 1587.

There was a brief reawakening of interest in transport improvements during the early years of the reign of Charles II, and the first Turnpike Act appears on the statute books in 1663. Temporary statutes were passed authorising the levying of rates for road repairs, but the turbulent years of the Popish Plot, the Exclusion Struggle, and the Revolution of 1688 brought about a halt, and it was in 1691 that the power to levy rates for road repairs was made permanent in 3 Wm. & Mary cap. 12. Between 1695 and 1700 four new turnpike acts were passed, and these were all similar in that Justices of the Peace were given the power to erect gates, collect tolls, appoint officials and supervise repairs. A completely new arrangement emerges in 1706 when a road was placed under the control of a group of 32 trustees, whose powers for repair, toll collection and so on, were, by and large, the same as those given to justices in earlier acts. By the time of the coming of the Hanoverians in 1714, the turnpike trust system had taken the place of the older powers and privileges granted in the 'Justice trust'.

It would seem that the 'highways' and 'byways' of the parish of Sopley were no better and no worse than those of other parishes within the county. Records of the Overseers, early deliberations of the Parish Council, and early photographs, all bear testimony to difficulties and hazards which must have created many problems for those responsible for upkeep and for those who had journeys to make, short or long. Nineteenth century records tell a full and sorry story of begging and sickness among 'strangers' on the road. At least their tribulations did not include the ever-present dangers inherent in the pedestrian use of roads without pavements in our own day.

Sopley's main road system today includes the B3347 from Christchurch to Ringwood, the road to Bransgore, minor road connections with Ripley, Shirley, the Lamb Inn and Winkton, and the Avon Causeway to Hurn and the

80: Roads and Traffic

West, which provides the only public vehicular crossing of the River Avon for several miles. There is also Priest Lane, Mill Lane, and a pleasing network of public footpaths. There was no one-way traffic system through the village until 1938.

Until the coming of the Bournemouth-Ringwood spur road in the 1960s, Sopley's main Christchurch-Ringwood road was numbered A338. Until the 1920s that part of the road which runs northwards towards Ringwood was called Avon Lane. The road to Bransgore was no more than a bridle path, and until the very early twentieth century the Avon Causeway was a private road, owned by Miss Fane of Avon. There were two other public crossings of the River Avon in the parish. One was close to Avon Tyrell where there was a bridge across the river which took equestrians and pedestrians to Sopley Common and Hurn railway station, via Pitt Farm. The other river crossing was part of the old road which left Avon Lane at a point opposite the cemetery gates, and the bridge came just a few yards to the north of Wild Weirs, where the mill-stream leaves the main river. On the west side of the river was a cottage which appears as Turnpike Cottage on the Tithe map of 1839.

There follow some extracts from the records which bear reference to Sopley road considerations, and a full report of the enquiry which preceded the setting up of a one-way system of traffic in 1938.

1896: A Parish Council proposition was passed, that Mr Whitaker be paid the cost of repairing the footpath called Church Way leading from Sopley to Ripley. A cheque was drawn for fourteen shillings.

1896: A letter from the clerk to the County Council was read, relating to the widening of the road near the cemetery and also part of the road between Mr Whitaker's and Mr Isiah Tuck at Avon.

1901: The clerk to the Parish was asked to write to the District Council, calling their attention to the bad state of the highway leading from Hurn station to Pitt House farm.

1902: Mr Goater brought forward the bad state of the Churchway gates on the bridle path leading from Court to Priest Lane.

1903: The Parish Council discussed the question of Miss Hamlyn Fane handing over the Avon Causeway to the public and Miss Fane's letter was read out:

> *"I have received a petition from residents in the Parish of Sopley asking me to give up my private road over the Avon to Hurn station to the District Council, and suggesting that the old road across the Avon at Tyrell's ford should be stopped. In reply I beg to point out that I will consent on the following conditions:*
>
> *1. That the handing over of the private road to the public, and the stopping of the Tyrell's ford road as a public road be carried out in a legal manner.*

81: Roads and Traffic

> 2. I, or my successors, be consulted about the design of the new bridge, with powers to reject.
> 3. That the District Council shall fence the road near the Hurn station adjoining the field now occupied by Lord Manners, so that the gate across the road may be taken away without throwing the field open to the road.
> 4. That the road shall continue in its present width."

Having discussed this letter the Sopley Parish Council then passed the following unanimous resolution:

> "Whereas the Public Highway known as Tyrell's Ford, situate in the Parish of Sopley and leading from a point on the public road 105 yards east of Hurn Station on the London and South Western Railway to the Christchurch and Ringwood road near the Avon Tyrell farm, is inconvenient and incommodious for the public, it is desirable and expedient that such road shall be closed, diverted, turned, or stopped up, and that a private road called or known as the Avon Causeway Toll Road situate in the Parish of Sopley from a point on the public road 210 yards east of the said Hurn Station to a point on the said Christchurch and Ringwood road opposite to the premises called or known as Court Farm, being more commodious and convenient for the public at large, therefore –
> This meeting of the Parish Council for the said Parish of Sopley do hereby deem it expedient for and consent to such highway of Tyrell's Ford Road being closed, or stopped up, and the private road of the Avon Causeway Road substituted therefor, as a public Highway to be repairable at the expense of the public at large."

1904: The clerk was instructed to write to the District Council and call their attention to the dangerous state of the approach to the footbridge in Fish Street, Ripley, and of the need for a rail or other protection on the right hand side of the bridge. Also to call the Council's attention to the waste of public money in the way the roadmen take 2-3 days to do one day's work, and the way in which the men so frequently leave their labour to visit public houses!

1905: The clerk brought the Council's attention to the unsafe condition of the bridge over the brook in Martin's Lane, the bad condition of Bogmoore Place and the unsafe condition of the footbridge at Ripley Brook.

1906: The question of the attempt to stop a footpath was discussed but as the Agent acknowledged the owner's inability to stop it after lengthy use, it was resolved that Miss Fane be asked to provide a stile at the south end of the path, instead of the ditch, bank and fence that at present cause an obstruction.

1907: Further complaints about the state of Priest Lane as far as Sopley Post Office (this was a very frequent complaint) and the state of the road near the Avon Causeway.

1907: A letter was authorised to be sent to the London and South Western Railway, calling their attention to the need of a gate being provided for intending passengers to gain access to Hurn Station.

1908: Complaints were received of the bad state of the main road from Bunnybrook to Court Farm.

1912: The clerk was authorised to write to Mr Walden to ask him to have the footpath near 'The Smith's Arms' repaired.

1931: The clerk reported that no answer had been received from the Hants and Dorset Bus Company as to the question of the provision of a Ripley bus but he understood that the chief difficulty in the way was the narrowness of the lane from Ripley to Sopley.

1937: A report in the *Christchurch Times* referred to the collapse of the Avon Causeway bridge, necessitating the rebuilding of it. It was suggested that flooding and the recent added weight of Macadam surfacing had brought about the collapse. The road was expected to be closed for about a month, during which time a new bridge would be constructed.

1938 September: Extracts from the *Christchurch Times* report on the Enquiry into the proposed one-way traffic system for Sopley: Mr Elton for the Council explained that the scheme was planned to operate over the A338 from the Woolpack Inn to the Smithy at Sopley, a distance of 227 yards, and over the unclassified road from the Smithy to the junction with the road to Bransgore, a distance of 257 yards. A census taken in 1935 of the traffic using the Ringwood-Christchurch road through Sopley, recorded that 8,220 vehicles passed during a week, and a census taken at Bisterne on the same road in 1937 recorded 9,271 vehicles within a week. It was stated when giving road measurements that there was no footpath on the classified road and that the road was tortuous, including an 'S' bend at Sopley Bridge and another immediately after the Smithy. The existing bus service operating on the Ringwood-Christchurch road already used the proposed one-way route.

The police supported the Council proposals, pointing out that between 1st September 1937 and 31st August 1938 there had been no fewer than four collisions at or near the bridge; there had been 5 accidents in the previous year and frequent damage to the bridge had been caused.

Mr H. Kemp-Welch, as a principal objector to the scheme, suggested by questions, that most of the accidents were due to fast driving. Col. the Lord

Manners, the local representative on the County Council, supported the scheme, but mentioned that the Parish Council were opposed to it. He admitted that the proposed measures would cause some inconvenience to residents of Sopley and agreed that a considerable number of the Bisterne 9,000 would have taken the Avon Causeway to Hurn.

Mr H. Kemp-Welch drew attention to the inconveniences which Sopley residents would suffer, and felt that the residents did not consider the road to be unnecessarily dangerous. "These roads are perfectly safe for vehicles which are driven at a reasonable speed," he said. "The excessive speed of cars is the whole cause of the trouble." He mentioned that the roads concerned in the enquiry contained the Post Office, the only telephone kiosk in the district, and the road to the church also joined one of the thoroughfares. A number of the Sopley services were used by people coming from Avon and adjoining villages, and the proposed scheme would entail significantly increased distances. He added that the normal village traffic consisted chiefly of horses and waggons and cattle, which added to the congestion of the unclassified thoroughfare, and these slow-moving vehicles would have to cross directly the line of traffic every time they passed through the village. To make a circuit of the village it was necessary also to negotiate the sharp corner by the Smithy, which would probably be too sharp for many of these cumbersome vehicles. Mr Kemp-Welch commented that buses had started using the proposed one-way system only when 'double-deckers' had come on to the route, and only then because the camber of the road near the bridge frequently caused the bus coming from Ringwood to collide with the roof of the Woolpack Inn. Furthermore, for children going to school the unclassified road had provided a haven of safety.

It was claimed that farmers would suffer serious inconvenience, especially at hay-making time. "It is impossible to do a tour round the village in under eight minutes, and in the farming business when, especially at hay-time, expediency was of importance, this restriction of traffic would be an unbearable burden." When asked by the police inspector about his view of a safe speed, Mr Kemp-Welch replied, "You can negotiate this village safely at speeds of up to fifteen miles an hour only."

Mr John Kemp-Welch, owner of Sopley Mill, spoke of the very considerable inconvenience he would suffer, and fears of an adverse effect on 'Woolpack' trade were expressed.

Several local farmers, including Messrs W. Farwell and D. Dalton, supported the objections of Mr Kemp-Welch, as did 'wheelwright' Vincent; and traders J.H. and A.H. Harrison had similar grievances. Mr C. Button said: "I live up that dilapidated County Council road called Priest Lane (laughter). I go to Bournemouth every day of the week, and I shall have to go twice as far."

84: Roads and Traffic

the promotion of one-way traffic would encourage faster driving which would increase the danger to pedestrians – especially to school-children.

Major J.D. Mills, M.P. did not think that the imposition of one-way traffic in Sopley was justified, but the Vicar of Sopley, Rev. D.F. Wright, considered that, in the interests of safety, one-way traffic would be a great boon.

The one-way system was installed, with a special dispensation allowing farm animals to ignore it. Two-way traffic was permitted on the short stretch of road between the 'Woolpack' and the Bransgore road junction, a concession which lends an element of chilling surprise to strangers on the course, a course on which no speed limits are imposed. Fifty years on, present residents of Sopley will have their own thoughts, born of half a century of increasingly heavy road traffic – juggernauts and all.

Flight over the Avon

It is a fairly common sight to see small binocular-busy groups in and around Sopley, intent on catching up with the rarer and sometimes more colourful birds that continue to invade the Parish boundaries. The Little Bustard has recently occasioned much interest, and a ferruginous duck on the Woolpack waters attracted the attention of enthusiasts in the springtime. The river, and its proximity to the sea, proves to be admirable "spotting and watching" territory, and the presence of a heronry gives a touch of regality to the scene. For who can fail to respond to the majestic heron, outsoaring the early-morning mist over the river meadows, its slow wing-beat and mournful cry an appropriate accompaniment to the patrol of an area rich in heritage, legends and all? By comparison perhaps, the discovery of a young green woodpecker of 1988 vintage, filling its belly with the ants of a superabundant year, is a more down-to-earth picture in every sense of the word. And there are the house-martins which, in the evening air, vie with the bats in their darting and weaving. These are just a few impressions of the present-day scene. As this is a glimpse of Sopley past and present, it is appropriate to refer to the feathered inhabitants of Sopley in another era and there follows a selection of Avon items from the Sporting Journals of the Second Earl of Malmesbury, who lived at Heron Court in the neighbouring Valley of the River Stour during the early decades of the 19th century.

Nov. 23 1807.	A sheldrake pitched under the weeping willow close to Avon Cottage.
Dec. 20 1809.	Dog caught a woodcock in a brake at Avon Cottage.
Apr. 12 1812.	Two woodcock were found at the Manor of Avon.
Dec. 4 1813.	Golden Plover seen on the Avon.
Dec. 10 1813.	Vast number of teal seen on the Avon ponds.
Sep. 29 1822.	Fine specimen of Osprey brought from Avon Cottage.
Jan. 17 1823.	Vast variety of fowl on the Avon including a Hooper.
Feb. 7 1823.	Crested cormorant on the Avon.
Mar. 11 1823.	More Hoopers on the Avon.
Dec. 7 1823.	Great Fishing Eagle seen on the Avon.
Feb. 21 1824.	Great Sea Eagle on the Avon.
Dec. 10 1825.	About twenty Golden Eyes on the Avon.
Jan. 27 1827.	Gadwell, golden eye, scaup, tufted duck – all on Avon.
Jan. 11 1832.	Bittern at Dudmoor.
Mar. 12 1832.	Pochards, tufted duck, teal & wigeon – all on Avon.
Dec. 24 1834.	Bittern at Avon Moor.

86: Flight over the Avon

Jan. 6 1836.	3 Gadwell on the Avon.
Feb. 6 1838.	**Between 50 and 60 Hoopers on the Avon.**
February 1840.	The long-continued floods brought a great quantity of wild fowl to the area. Large numbers of duck, gadwell, flight wigeon, teal. A falcon was observed in constant pursuit. A duck and wigeon found lying dead, side by side. Probably, chased by the falcon, there had been a panic collision.

The above are extracts from *Half a Century of Sport in Hampshire* published in 1905 in the *"Country Life" Library of Sport*.

The Work of the Parish Council

The first meeting of the Sopley Parish Council took place on January 28th 1894 at the British School in Sopley. The earliest pages of the Council minute books however are concerned with the activities of the Burial Board. A letter addressed to the Incumbent of Sopley from Whitehall, and dated 3rd March 1881, ordains that no new burial ground shall be opened in the parish without the previous approval of one of Her Majesty's principal Secretaries of State. The same letter forbids any burials in the churchyard at Sopley after September 30th 1881, other than in existing vaults and walled graves. Burials in the Independent Church at Ripley were to discontinue immediately.

This prompted a vestry meeting at Sopley on March 25th 1881, at which it was decided to seek a new burial ground in the parish, and that a Burial Board of seven be chosen forthwith.

Two possible sites for a cemetery were chosen, one in a field adjoining a cottage occupied by W. Barrow in Avon, and in case this should be objected to, a second one was suggested in a field opposite the already disused causeway to Herne. A government inspector duly inspected both sites in June, and reported that either would be suitable, but he preferred the second one because it was nearer to the Parish Church, no further from Ripley Independent Church, and free from the potential nuisance value of tree roots. It was also cheaper.

It was decided to surround the new cemetery with a brick wall, and a lychgate was constructed. At a vestry meeting held in July 1881 it was resolved to ask for the consent of the parish to the borrowing, on the security of the rates, a sum not exceeding £500 for the purchase and enclosure of a parish cemetery, together with a covered gateway.

In the ensuing months frequent meetings dealt with the many financial considerations involved, drew up a table of dues to be paid at the cemetery, and appointed a gravedigger and maintenance man. Eventually the 87th and last meeting of the Burial Board was held and its work was formally handed over to the first meeting of the Parish Council.

The minutes of Sopley Parish Council meetings since the closing years of the 19th century reveal the presentation to them of an ever-increasing variety of problems and considerations. Their constant concern with the development of highways and byways is recorded elsewhere in this book in the chapter on roads. For the rest it is easy to discern the gradual acceleration into the more complicated life of twentieth century England.

High-spirited, and sometimes misguided, youth evoked a familiar pattern of concern and condemnation. Proceedings of the local magistrates' courts contain evidence of boisterous behaviour rather than of violence. In 1895 the local council decided to petition for the provision of a constable for the parish, and for occasional "informal" visits to the parish of uniformed upholders of law and order.

Pests of other kinds come into the reckoning at fairly frequent intervals. The problem of sparrows at the Crystal Palace and the Duke of Wellington's reply to Queen Victoria's request for advice on the subject are well-known nationally. In Sopley Parish, in 1898, the Council is entreated to take steps against the Sopley sparrows which are causing serious damage to local farmers. Nearly twenty years later, in 1917, the following scale of rewards was current in the parish:

> *Threepence a dozen for heads of fully-fledged house sparrows.*
> *Twopence a dozen for heads of unfledged house sparrows.*
> *One penny a dozen for eggs of house sparrows.*

In 1931 urgent attention is called to a plague of rats near Harpway Lane.

Periodically the Council received complaints concerning the state of the allotments at Shirley, and for a time a certain amount of confusion appeared to prevail over the renting of these. In 1928 a letter from Lord Manners to the Council refers to the latter's enthusiasm for the provision of a recreation ground at Ripley. Lord Manners wrote:

> *"I have received the resolution of the parish meeting as to a recreation ground at Ripley, and am anxious to do all in my power to assist in the matter."*

The provision of more and more local services is a frequent item on the agenda. In 1901 a circular letter was received from the Local Government Board concerning free libraries, an isolation hospital, and extra postal services. Developments of this kind often brought about painful modifications of time-honoured practice. In 1905 this heartfelt petition to the Postmaster General is recorded:

> *"An alteration in the rural postal arrangements for this locality has been thought advisable for the better delivery of letters. In connection with this however we the Parish Council for the Parish of Sopley and the inhabitants regret to hear of the contemplated removal at the end of the present month from this district of the Postman, Mr F.G. Freeman. We can with confidence and satisfaction testify to his punctuality, civility, and the capable manner in which he has, for nearly 25 years, discharged his duties. We would respectfully remind*

89: The Work of the Parish Council

you that his removal will mean the breaking up of his home and other life-long ties and we trust that you might be able to make arrangements as may lead to his retention on his present round for the few remaining years as may be left to him, and thus he may continue to serve the population of this district which so much wishes to retain him as Postman. Trusting you may be able to grant the Prayer of this petition."

The Parish Fire Engines Act, requiring that due attention be given to this ever-present need for adequate provision, was passed in 1898 and thirty years later came a letter from the Bournemouth Fire Brigade Company, regretting that it was unable to answer Sopley calls. In 1930 the first telephone kiosk was installed in Sopley and in 1936 application was made for the provision of further kiosks at Ripley crossroads and outside the New Queen at Avon.

The provision of Sunday train services was the subject of occasional pressure. In 1907, in response to yet another plea, the railway agreed to run two Sunday trains between Ringwood and Christchurch for an experimental period. The experiment was not successful; but this did not deter the Council from sending, the following year, a letter of appreciation to Mr Finch, stationmaster at Hurn for thirty-four years. He was presented with a purse of gold containing eight pounds, three and sixpence. It was during 1907 also that a request was made for the re-establishment of a Parish Pound; this was not persevered with because of the costs involved. A request for the moving of the local polling station from the National School at Sopley to the Council school at Ripley was more favourably received.

Demands for money from the Overseers of the Poor Rate are a constant item in the pages of the Council minutes. Britain in 1988 is in a ferment over financial reform. In 1906 Sopley Parish Council passed the following resolution which speaks for itself:

"This meeting of the Parish Council of Sopley views with alarm the increase of the Poor Rate – principally due to the abnormal demands of the County Council and that this meeting protests against same, and urges the County Council to confer with local managers and to delegate, as far as possible, all work of repair to schools, increased accommodation and other work requiring close attention to the urban or other local bodies for their supervision and control."

Education

The nineteenth and early twentieth century story of education in Sopley parish is largely concerned with three schools. In reading such written records as are available, a vivid impression of some of the hopes and fears of these times can be obtained. Rivalry and acrimony are notable ingredients when the Established Church and Nonconformity enter the lists. Financial poverty is a prominent contributor to the problems of the day. Conscientious service to the cause of the young is never far to seek, whether devoted to the glamour of the British Empire, or more basically to the brains and bellies of the pupils. Inspections of work are regular and conscientious. And character and life are everywhere: the daily ride to school on a donkey, the provision of supplementary help to the telegraph service of the day by the simple expedient of coverting a willing pupil to the ranks of messenger boys when outlying addresses were involved, the regular skirmishing (often more verbal than physical) between those of different religious persuasions. The fear of Hell-fire lingers in the air, fed by the awe-inspiring accuracy of the local schoolmaster; the very day after he had issued a solemn warning that the devil comes for naughty children, the church alongside was struck by lightning!

Two schools existed in the village, less than a mile apart. One closed in 1895 when the Sopley County Primary School was opened at Ripley, and of its buildings on the Ringwood Road north of the Post Office, only a few bricks remain. The other, next door to the church, ended its existence in 1944, and its buildings now provide living accommodation for a small number of people.

The Ringwood Road school was known as the British School. It was built for 126 pupils in 1828 and enlarged in 1852, and was Nonconformist in its associations; the minister, Rev. Mr Howarth, was a frequent visitor, riding his bicycle from 'The Manse' and towing Mrs Howarth in a bath chair behind him. The daily average attendance here was 94 as recorded in 1890.

Some of the names of the 'Masters' of the British School are discoverable: 1859, Richard Dundrell; 1871, Mr Eversden; 1878, Mr and Mrs Sansom; 1895, Charles Mason. When the school was closed in 1895, Charles Mason went to the new school at Ripley and was still there as late as 1923. The new school was officially opened in 1896, with its first Sopley School board under the chairmanship of Lord Manners. Included on the board were local farmers and the miller from Sopley. There were 59 children on the roll and by 1902 this number had increased to 84. They were taught by a staff of three, headmaster and wife and one other teacher. Following the passing of the 1902 Education Act Hampshire County Council took over the school with virtually the same board.

More records of the National School exist. It was built at a cost of three

91: Education

hundred pounds and opened in 1833. A list of masters and mistresses here includes: 1859, Mr and Mrs Barrow; 1867, Mr and Mrs William Jennings; 1890, Mr and Mrs Joseph Parker; 1894, Mr P. Franklin and Miss Alice Franklin; 1911, Mr George Baker; 1915, Mrs L. Howcroft; 1923, Mrs K. Robinson. When the National School closed in the summer of 1944, words of praise abounded for the Mistress, Miss Baker. The average attendance was 60 during the 1890s; by 1911 this number had shrunk to 49, and by 1944 there were only 7 left. A study of documents in the church's keeping, together with early magazines and the local press, helps to feed the recollections of those who attended this lively centre of learning.

In February 1867 Mrs Fane and Mrs Lucas gave a red cloak to each of the girls attending the national day school. These cloaks were worn for the first time on the first Sunday after Epiphany and it is reported that they looked bright and warm in the midst of the snow. The schools appear to have been inspected annually, and a few extracts from the reports of Her Majesty's Inspectors will reveal that considerable optimism was often expressed, but compliments were by no means indiscriminate:

April 1867: Rev. J.H. Nutt spent several hours examining every class. The children are in good order, and two upper classes are making very fair progress.

June 1868: Rev. N. Mitchell H.M.I. visited and expressed himself pleased with the school's condition. This being the second good report since Mr Jennings became master, he is now qualified to sit for the Government Certificate at the next examination, after which the school, being under a certificated teacher, can obtain a Parliamentary grant. A summary of the report, couched in suitably enigmatic terms, was: As much is being done as can be expected.

1869: It was reported that there should be fewer failures in Arithmetic, and 'the offices' for the two sexes require to be more effectually separated.

1870: My Lords hope that the managers will at once make the partition between the privies effectual. Discipline was good and the children had passed fairly well on the whole. More attention should be given to the instruction of the lower classes. Their R's were hardly satisfactory. *In August 1871, the National School reopened after a month's closure for scarletina and for the school to be disinfected. No Harvest holiday – the school to remain open until Christmas.*

May 1876: The school was examined by H.M.I. George Gordon. 75 children were present, of whom 6 were infants; and 42 elder scholars had made 250 attendances and so were qualified to be presented for examination. The inspector was much pleased with the knowledge of geography shown by the first class and with the girls', needlework. "Mr Jennings has his school in good order and continues to show good results."

March 1880: Much local pride was felt at this time when the pass list of the pupil-teachers' examination in religious knowledge was issued. 482 pupil-teachers and monitors in Hampshire and the Isle of Wight were examined. 61 gained first class and of these, Florence Hatcher, pupil-teacher at Sopley School, was placed first in her year. She was descibed as especially distinguished and was awarded an extra prize of ten shillings for Prayer-book subjects. Clara Gaterell, a candidate in the same school, was second in the first class.

Very early in the National School's history there was agitation brought about by the appearance of a claim to the site on which the school stood. It was feared that if the claim was legally substantiated then the property might be used for some sectarian purpose, a development next door to the church which would have been particularly abhorrent to the curate at the time, Rev. Douglas Veitch. His strongly expressed fears were set at rest.

Tentative experiments in further education are revealed when in October 1867 Mr Jennings, the National schoolmaster, announced his willingness to instruct classes of labouring men or lads during the winter; and in 1880 evening classes for men and lads were advertised at the National School on Tuesday and Thursday evenings. Fee – one penny a week.

At varying times considerable efforts were made to improve the school's attendance record, as may be seen from the wording of a rule agreed upon by the School Committee in 1869:

> *"Labouring men may have their children taught at this school on payment in advance of one shilling a quarter. This covers everything except books. Any child may pay two pence into a clothing club every Monday to which one penny will be added when the child is in regular attendance the week before, and the home and Sunday lessons have been well said."*

In this same year the Master's salary was forty pounds per annum, with the addition of about three pounds a quarter from a government grant.

While Sopley was without a village hall, school premises often played a decisive part in community life. Let this brief description of a missionary tea-party, attended by seventy people, and held at the National School in 1880, serve to represent a host of functions held in scholastic premises over a period of a hundred years:

93: Education

"Mrs Jennings superintended all the arrangements, which were excellent. After tea, the Vicar gave an account of the conversion of Abyssinia, and the work, stranger than fiction, of Mr Duncan in British Columbia. Rev. W. Scott gave an account of his experiences of clerical life in South Australia, and Rev. H.M. Wilkinson spoke of the great support every Christian was bound to give to the propagation of the Gospel. Some Mexican and Burmese idols were exhibited."

Sopley School children 1927.
Back row (l to r): Alec Harrison, Bob Beaton, Joe Stone, Steve Beaton, Arthur Gilbert, Bill Beaton.
Middle row (l to r): Bob Harrison, Hilda Minty, Walter Cottrill, Bob Penny, Marjorie Denton, Hubert Harrison, John Brown, Annie Cole, Ken Padwicke, Dorothy Thorner, Dick Hodder, May Berryman, John Lane, Sue Burt, Len Newman, Hilda Minty, John Northover, Grace Eldon, Bob Eldon, Ron Dunford, Reg Harrison, Lil Brown.
Seated (l to r): John Stone, Dot Miles, Vera Hodder, May Penny, Phyllis Gilbert, Phyllis Harrison, Emily Miles.
Photgraph loaned by Mary Russell.

Some Sopley Worthies

BENJAMIN HARDY 1844–1931.

Benjamin Hardy was born at Nottingham in 1844. It is said that the family is distantly connected with the Wessex author, Thomas Hardy, and were descendants of Nelson's Captain Hardy. In his early life Mr Hardy proved his mettle by running away to sea and for a score of years he experienced many adventures in the Far East. Later he acted as an instructor in seamanship at Dartmouth, and then he was in H.M. Prison Service at Portland.

When Mr Hardy's grandfather went to live at Studland, he is said to have been associated with smugglers. The story is told of a trapdoor in his grandfather's house which led to a store of contraband goods. On one occasion a visit was paid to the house by the Preventive Men, and Mr Hardy's grandmother sat upon a stool over the trapdoor and thus hid it from their notice.

Mr Hardy went to live at Sopley and was much respected in the district. For some fourteen years he was churchwarden and school manager for the Rev. J.F. Vallings who described him as a "just man". He was generally known in the Avon Valley as "the grand old man of Sopley".

JAMES FREDERICK VALLINGS. 1854–1929.
VICAR OF SOPLEY. 1888–1929.

Reference to the work and human qualities of the Rev. J.F. Vallings during the forty-one years of his ministry at Sopley are so numerous and so complimentary that there is no doubt about the very high regard in which he was held.

He was presented with the living of Sopley by the Dean and Chapter of Canterbury at the beginning of 1888 and he took up residence in the village in March of that year. He preached his 41st anniversary sermon in the parish church on the Sunday preceding his death when he took the same text as he did in his first local sermon.

James Vallings was a man of many parts. A fine athlete in his youth, he was a pugilist of some renown and a great supporter of the local cricket and football clubs, for which he lent a field near the vicarage. One of today's very elderly gentlemen relates that he always knew exactly how the vicar would greet him, according to the season of the year: "How's the Cricket?", "How's the Football?" A tireless worker for the Red Triangle Club and the Sopley Flower Show, he was also the author of several books, including *The Severing Sword*, *Double Siege* and *Jesus, the Divine Man*.

95: Some Sopley Worthies

Mainly due to the vicar's perseverance, the belfry at St Michael's Church was restored and the bells recast as a memorial to those of the parish who fell in the Great War. The bells were silent from Armistice Day until December 1925 when the work was completed and the rehung bells (dating from 1784) were dedicated by the Bishop of Southampton.

Vallings married Lily Cadogan Chanter, daughter of the Vicar of Ilfracombe and niece of Charles Kingsley. There were nine children of whom one son was killed in the Great War and another lost his life in an accident in New Zealand. To a small boy pumping air into the church organ, Mrs Vallings at the keys could be an awesome and frightening proposition; her face would appear round the side of the organ and she would hiss "More wind, more wind!" at intervals during the service. She was a familiar figure to all local residents in her pony and trap on the road from Sopley to Christchurch and back. The vicar and his wife were free and generous in the loan of their home at the vicarage at many times throughout the year. Latterly Mr Vallings found the large garden there increasingly difficult to cope with. His successor, a keen gardener, took over a semi-wilderness. When the time came to clear the long grass from the large south lawn, an ancient lawn-mower was found bogged down in the midst of it.

The widespread affection in which Mr Vallings was held is reflected in the party which was given for him at the Schoolhouse in January 1923, on the occasion of his 69th birthday. The chair was taken by Major E.J. Stevens O.B.E., from Chiltley House, and presentations were made on behalf of the villagers by Mr Benjamin Hardy. These included an up-to-date BSA bicycle, an easy chair for man and wife, a box of cigarettes, a set of water-proof garments and a purse containing the balance of the money collected. The bicycle was provided by a village tradesman, Mr A.J. Harrison.

At the vicar's funeral in 1929 the Rural Dean (Canon W.H. Gay) at Christchurch referred to him as author, scholar, saint and gentleman. It is reported that the Dissenters of the parish combined in sending a wreath of their own, and the bell-ringers paid tribute to his memory by ringing muffled peals before and after the service, when they rang a quarter peal of Grandsire Doubles, 120 changes. The bell-ringers were: B. Kendell, W. Freeman, E.H. Harrison, G. Nicholson, F.E. Blake and G. Preston, and the bearers were: H.R. Berryman, S. Beaton, J. Murray, A. Lane, H. Harrison and F. Blake. Three years later, when oak panelling was assembled in the sanctuary as a memorial to him, the Archdeacon of Winchester said that he had always found the Rev. Vallings a living example of St Paul's nine fruits of the spirit: love, joy, peace, long-suffering, gentleness, goodness, faith, meekness and self-control.

JOHN KEMP-WELCH. 1859–1939.

Sopley has seldom enjoyed the luxury of a resident Lord of the Manor; but the presence of a squire, and a squire's residence and park, enriched the life of the community for several generations. From the later years of the 19th century until the outbreak of the Second World War, John Kemp-Welch provided a strain of ruling leadership which functioned in a well-nigh perfect setting for a squire's domain. The church on the hill, the ancient bridge and inn, the thatched and clustered cottages, the brook, the park and its beautiful trees, and the imposing, if not breath-taking, squire's house, which has now been demolished.

'Mr John' entered the scene as a young man, his father John having purchased the estate from the executors of the late Mr William Tice in 1868. Amongst the earliest Kemp-Welch Sopley documents is a small notebook of the 1870s, containing ornithological notes written by the young man as he explored the neighbouring woods and fields. In those days Christchurch was predominant in the district; Bournemouth was remote and virtually unknown. The squire's remarkable contribution to local and county government and administration seem almost part of a single-minded dedication to keep Sopley intact. This was surely always very close to the centre of his heart. Whenever there was cause for widespread celebration he was there in the middle of it; a photograph from the earlier years of the 20th century shows a giant marquee set up in Sopley Park, full of long tables meticulously and beautifully laid for a local banquet. The seats are unoccupied, yet they somehow appear to be accommodating generations of his flock.

One of his lasting and most happy gifts to the village came about at the time of his Golden Wedding in June 1934. He supervised the conversion of an ancient barn in the centre of the village into a splendid assembly hall. The precise date of origin of the barn is unknown, but cut into its brickwork is the inscription – R. Wright 1768. The day of the Golden Wedding celebrations was heralded by a merry peal of bells and the arrival of numerous gifts and good wishes. In the evening a great entertainment was held in the assembly hall, attended by 150 tenants. Among them was the oldest inhabitant of Sopley at that time, Mr Eli Butler, aged 91. He was village shoemaker in his day, and Mr Kemp-Welch, in a speech full of reminiscences, mentioned that Eli had made him his first catapult. His accuracy with it quite exceeded his expectations, for he killed the family cat, to the consternation of himself and those around him. One of the chief communal gifts from the village to Mr and Mrs Kemp-Welch was a handsome reading glass. There were many speeches, including one from Brigadier General Stewart who thanked the squire on behalf of the British Legion, and thanked him also on behalf of the Bowling Club for the splendid bowling green which he had given to the club from within his own demesne.

Mr John Kemp-Welch, JP (for nearly fifty years) died at Sopley Park on 19th March 1939 in his 81st year. At St Michael's Church, and at Sopley Cemetery, guards of honour were formed by Christchurch and Ringwood police; the Avon Valley Boy Scouts were also on parade. Great crowds attended the funeral and representative wreaths were received from a wide variety of groups and organisations: Sopley British Legion, West Hants Water Co., officers of the New Forest Division of the Hampshire Constabulary, South Avon and Stour Agricultural Society, N.F.U. (Ringwood Branch), Sopley Social Club, Sopley Bowling Club, Sopley Cricket Club, Flower Show, Christchurch Justices, Sopley Vicar and parishioners, Trustees of Talbot Village, Officers and Brethren of the Loyal River Avon Lodge of Oddfellows, Sopley C.E. School, the garden staff, Sopley Parish Council.

The coffin was borne on a horse-drawn farm waggon which slowly wound its way down the slope from the church and up the road to Sopley Cemetery: foundation member of Hampshire County Council, Chairman Sopley Rural District Council, County Magistrate at Christchurch and Ringwood for twelve years, Chairman of West Hampshire Water Company (one of its original share holders), thirty five years Chairman of the old Board of Guardians, member of Highways and Sanitary Boards.

As Europe thundered to the tramp of armed men, an era in the history of Sopley was ending, in dignity and peace.

EDWARD HARRY HARRISON. 1894–1983.
(From notes supplied by Mrs Doris Harrison.)

Harry Harrison, as he was affectionately known on all sides, was the seventh son of a seventh son, but there appeared to be nothing particularly supernatural about his considerable and varied abilities. On his mother's side he was a great-grandson of William Fey, a refugee from the French Revolution, who established himself as an agriculturalist and public benefactor in Burley. His father came of farming stock from Hale, near Fordingbridge.

Harry's father died when he was very young, leaving his mother with seven children to bring up. Jack, aged 16, carried on his father's blacksmith business and his mother kept cows. The children were brought up on milk and home-made butter and cheese. A family pig was salted down for the winter and the family grew its own vegetables. They thrived, did well in their respective careers, and lived to a good age, all except a twin who died at the age of nine years.

Harry attended Sopley School when it was next door to the parish church and left there at the age of thirteen. At this tender age he started work at Carter's Dairies in Christchurch, but the job was not to his liking and he soon found work with Mooring-Aldridge and Haydon, solicitors in the same town.

The First World War broke out when he was in his 20th year, and he enlisted, together with many Sopley pals. He and his brother Albert went off to India with the 5/7 Hampshire Regiment, to which Mr Kemp-Welch was commissioned. To young men who had never been further than Bournemouth and Salisbury, it must have been similar to a journey to the moon in later times. During his service of nearly five years abroad, Harry was at Basra, guarding prisoners of war, and at one time Gandhi was one of the prisoners in his charge.

Homesickness overtook him, probably at the time of his 21st birthday and he literally sat down by the waters of Babylon and wept for Sopley. His sister sent a Christmas cake a little later in the year but it was green when it reached him. At the end of the war he contracted peritonitis. While he was lying very ill in hospital, his battalion marched past on their way home singing "Take me back to dear old Blighty". This was not calculated to cheer the sick man up. Happily he made a good recovery and soon the train deposited him at Salisbury station, from whence he set out for Sopley, his service career behind him.

Harry rejoined his old firm of solicitors in Christchurch and soon moved to Bournemouth where he met his future wife, Doris Frodsham. They were married at Richmond Congregational Church in 1933. About this time he purchased a motor-cycle to take him to and from his work, whatever the weather; usually his sister rode pillion passenger as far as Boscombe.

About 1936 he left Mooring Aldridge and Haydon and took up a job as managing clerk with Messrs Laceys, solicitors in Bournemouth. Although his circumstances did not allow him to take articles, his services and advice were frequently sought by those more highly qualified than himself. He was ever ready to offer his services to people at any time of the day or evening. Often his evening meal lay drying up in the oven while he wrestled with problems brought to his door. His widow recalls that some of the people involved did pay for his advice with an occasional pheasant. She recalls the day when he had had eight or ten teeth extracted and was still spitting blood when someone telephoned to say that her mother had died and left three hundred pounds under the mattress. Would Harry please come and look after it? Despite the pleas of his wife he insisted on going.

During the Second World War he was second in command of Burton Home Guard and helped to guard the small bridge below Sopley Church. This area was looked upon as a likely landing place for enemy parachutists.

His enquiring mind led him to turn his attention to many fields of knowledge. He went to night school at Bournemouth College, learning shorthand, typing and accountancy. While in Basra he had tried to learn Arabic and when wireless broadcasts began he tried his hand at French.

Harry Harrison gave a long lifetime of service to the local church. He was choir boy, choir master, organist, bell-ringer, churchwarden and treasurer. He would spend hours going through old church records, helping to find ancestors for visiting Americans and Australians. His bell-ringing was also well-known at Christchurch Priory, for sixty years. He was happy and proud to receive a testimonial from the Vicar and Church Council at Sopley for eighty years of service to the church.

The list of his active involvements is seemingly endless. He was President of the Sopley and Bransgore British Legion and President of Sopley Oddfellows. He started the Burton Residents Association and became its first President. He worked tirelessly for the acquisition of playing fields for Burton village and obtained the Duke of Edinburgh's help in securing them. The area was very boggy and the Bournemouth Football Association would not allow their teams to play there; this meant Burton had to play 'away'. When the Christchurch Bypass was being constructed, Harry obtained loads of displaced earth from the Council to fill up the boggy places.

Harry and his wife were able to celebrate their Golden Wedding shortly before his death. A very worthy and beloved son of Sopley.

100: Some Sopley Worthies

WILLIAM TICE. 1792–1866.

William Tice was born at Ware in Hertfordshire. He came into the Sopley area at an early age and in 1843 he bought 81 acres, including Sopley Park House, from George James Brandon Willis. Having received a liberal education and having inherited a considerable fortune, he secured a large circle of friends, and quickly established a good reputation among his neighbours. William was a member of a staunch Nonconformist family and became well-known as a friend of civil and religious liberty.

The scale of his contributions to local life is reflected in the frequency with which his name is recorded in positions of responsibility and authority. He was a stern upholder of Commoners' rights and at the time of the building of the Christchurch-Ringwood Railway he was elected to both the Sopley and Avon Committees who were chosen to safeguard the interests of rights on Sopley Common. Almost inevitably it seems, his name appears as foreman of the local Coroner's juries. He is careful to submit the necessary claim forms (there were claim forms in the mid 19th century as well!) for rights in or over the New Forest. Nor was the beautiful park land which he had purchased jealously preserved from public enjoyment. Accounts of large Temperance fêtes held there with his blessing echo with joyfulness.

He was a candidate for the representation of Christchurch Borough in Parliament, perhaps more for the purpose of having an opportunity of expounding his strongly-held principles than in expectaion of a successful candidature. His funeral took place on Wednesday 20th June 1866 at the Independent Chapel, Christchurch. The Rev. Joseph Fletcher gave an address and summarised his comments in the words: "An honourable and useful life, crowned by a quiet and peaceful death."

PURTON SPARKS. 1893–1987.

Purton Sparks was born in the village of Shirley in Sopley Parish. He went to school in Sopley village and more often than not he made his way on donkey-back; he would tether his mount in the old barn attached to the Vicarage and wend his way on foot over the Woolpack Bridge and up the slope.

His father was a smallholder and his grandfather, Levi Purton, was a well-known gamekeeper. It may be said therefore that the life's profession upon which he embarked was already in his blood. When he was thirteen he began his career as a kennel boy at Avon Tyrell, under head-keeper George Miller. His main duty was to look after seven retrievers, for which services he was paid five shillings a week. Purton married a local girl, Nellie, who was the daughter of George Dean, for many years keeper to Major Cecil Mills at Bisterne.

When the Great War began in 1914, he lost no time in joining up. Lord Manners wished him to join his old regiment, the Grenadier Guards. He was not quite tall enough however and enrolled in the Hampshire Regiment. He saw service under General Allenby in Egypt, and was wounded in the leg by a dum-dum bullet outside Jaffa in Palestine; the wound was to trouble him on and off for most of his long life. This did not stop him from becoming a very enthusiastic member of Bransgore Home Guard in World War 2.

After the war he returned to Avon Tyrell and continued his gamekeeper's career. The shoot at Avon Tyrell comprised some 3,000 acres and Purton had control over large areas of it. He became known as a very adept trapper, a business which he learned in a hard school. He recalled that in his early days he once set fifty traps for rats, but one of the keepers sprang them all and told him eloquently to set them again in the correct manner! References to rats are quite common in the old Avon Valley records.

Among the famous people who came to shoot at Avon Tyrell Purton used to speak vividly of a very good shot whom the keepers knew as the "Black Prince"; in reality he was the Maharajah of Bikaner. He recalled that the Maharajah always had three loaders and made a point of using brass-cased cartridges. He believed that brass cases avoided dampness, and so perhaps facilitated the work of the loaders.

He spoke of partridges being much more abundant on the estate in his early days and recalls the shooting of woodcock at Avon Tyrell; the 19th century presence of woodcock there is also testified to in the Shooting Journals of the second Earl of Malmesbury.

102: Some Sopley Worthies

In the later years of his retirement, after the death of his wife, Purton Sparks was a familiar figure in his sun hat and chair outside the front door of No. 16, Sopley. There was always a cheerful wave and a twinkle in his eye for the passerby, and he reminisced colourfully and with a great sense of humour. He used to attribute his rheumatism to the fact that he would take his boots off to walk through the wet grass so as not to disturb the cooped hens and the pheasant chicks when locking them up for the night. For a man who had lived so many years, his memory was remarkable. He could quote without hesitation the titles of books written sixty years ago by the Rev. Vallings; he recalled vividly the cameraderie in his first barrack room in 1914. He told of his discovery of a spring at Ripley and of how an aeroplane crashed only two hundred yards from where he was standing in the fields in World War 2. His face broadened into a mischievous smile as he remembered the gamekeepers' habit of slipping into the 'local' for a quickie during working hours. One of the party would act as 'cave', and with the landlord's connivance an escape route was available via the back door and a hole in the garden hedge, should the boss appear at an inconvenient moment. What more human way could there be of disappearing from the scene?

TWO FAMOUS SOLDIERS AT REST IN SOPLEY CHURCHYARD.
John, first Lord Keane. 1781–1844.

In the southern part of Sopley churchyard may be found the altar tomb of Lieutenant General Lord Keane, G.C.B. and G.C.R. who "served and fought for his country in the four quarters of the globe".

He was born at Belmont, Co. Waterford, and in 1794 he was appointed captain in a new regiment raised on Beresford estates. In 1813 he joined Wellington's army and was head of a brigade of the Third Division at Vittoria. Promoted to Major General in 1814, he was severely wounded in an unsuccessful attack on New Orleans in 1815. In the same year he was created KCB Gold Cross and two clasps for his service in Martinique, Vittoria, Pyreneés, the Nive, and Toulouse.

From 1823-1830 he commanded troops in Jamaica, during which time he was promoted to Lieutenant General. In the following year he became Colonel of the 68th Light Infantry.

Appointed Commander-in-Chief, Bombay 1833-39, in 1838 the Bombay government sent a division under Keane into Scinde to coerce the Ameers.

At Kandahar on 8th May 1839, in the presence of the British Envoy, Keane and the British force, the Shah, Soojah, was placed on the throne. Kabul was

103: Some Sopley Worthies

occupied on 7th August. Keane was made GCB at the end of the year and raised to the peerage by the title of Baron Keane of Ghuznee (or Ghazni), with a pension for his own and two succeeding lives and was granted an honourable augmentation of his family arms; he also received the thanks of Parliament and of the directors of the East India Company. *Ghazni is a famous city in Afghanistan on the direct road from Kandahar to Kabul. It was brought into the limelight again by the news of its capture by the British Army under Sir J. Keane, 23rd July 1839.*

General Keane died at Burton Lodge on 26th August 1844, aged 63.

General Sir George Harry Smith Willis. 1822–1900.

The organ in Sopley Parish Church bears the inscription: "Presented to the Church and Parish of Sopley by General Sir George Willis GCB in memory of old friends, AD 1900." Almost opposite the organ in the south transept is a mural tablet which reads:

To the memory of
General Sir George Harry Smith Willis.
Born 11 November 1822. Died 29 November 1900.
Grand Cross of the Order of the Bath.
Grand Officer of the Legion of Honour.
Knight of the Order of St John of Jerusalem.
Knight of the Ottoman Order of the Osmanieh.
Chevalier of the Order of the Medjidie.
Commander of the Tunisian Military Order.
Officer of the Italian Order for Military Valour.
Recipient of the three British medals
The Sultan's Medal and the Khedive's Bronze Star.

"Not far away a boy was born to fair prosperity,
But grew up struggling hard with fell adversity.
Then entering in the world's rough race
He won at length a foremost place
_ and then he died.
Behold before you all that remains of life's short span and glory."

104: Some Sopley Worthies

Although the details of the 'fell adversity' of his youth appear to be hidden from the researcher's view, this chronicle of his many decorations bears vivid testimony to his very distinguished military service.

He was the only son of G.B. Willis of Sopley Park, and was twice married – first to Eliza, daughter of George Morgan MP and then to Ada, daughter of Sir John Neeld.

In 1841 he joined the 44th Foot, serving in Malta, Corfu, Jamaica, Nova Scotia and Canada. He landed in the Crimea with the Light Division and fought in the battles of Balaklava and Inkerman and in the two assaults on the Redan. He was slightly wounded on several occasions.

He was appointed DAQMG at HQ Crimea, and afterwards AQMG of the 4th Division until the end of the Crimean War. In 1856 he was with French in Africa and subsequent appointments included QMG Gibraltar 1858-59, AG Malta 1859-64, QMG South Division 1866-71 and AQMG HQ 1872-75.

He commanded the 1st Division in the Egyptian expedition of 1882 and was wounded at the Battle of Tel-el-Kebir. It was at this battle also that tradition has it that he took a flag from Arabi's tent with his own hands and this trophy was one of two flags that formerly flanked his memorial tablet in Sopley Church. General Willis gave the window in the south transept as a thanksgiving for the successes of his career; in his will he left financial coverage for the upkeep of Willis memorials and grave, with the balance to be allocated to the needs of the poor. General Willis's tomb, very simply inscribed, lies in the churchyard between the south transept and the new vestry.

The War to End All War 1914 – 1918

In the middle of the nave of Sopley Parish Church two war memorials may be seen facing each other. On the one tablet of stone are the names of forty-four men of the parish who gave their lives in the First World War and on the other, ten names of those Sopley Parish men who died in the service of their country during the Second World War. If the years between the two Armistices be counted it will be found that they add up to 21, the old, magical 'coming of age' number. A considerable percentage of the armed forces in 1935-45 was made up of men and women who were born during the carnage of the War that was called 'Great'. Memorials to the fallen abound in city, town, and village centres, and in churches. The names constitute a brotherhood of sacrifice, whether in tens of thousands at the Menin Gate, or in tens at Sopley Church. Let their names speak for themselves in silence now, for 'Silence alone can speak to Death in Death's own dignity'.

ROLL OF HONOUR 1914-1918: Frank Barrow, Fred Barrow, Sam Barrow, S. Barrow, P. Bollom, G. Bramble, J. Bramble, F. Brewer, E. Burt, T. Burt, G. Carpenter, G. Chilcott, G. Churchill, F. Clapcott, H. Clapcott, C. Dean, D. Dowland, H. Dowland, J. Dowland, C. Gilbert, G. Gilbert, S. Gilbert, P. Harkness, C. Hill, W. Hook, W. Hunt, W. Kendall, E. Linington, E. Lyde, Hon J. Manners, F. Marsh, G. Marsh, H. Marsh, F. Osment, P. Pope, J. Potts, J. Ransome, H. Street, P. Thick, J. Thorner, R. Vallings, J. Whitfield, G. Whitlock, H. Whitlock.

ROLL OF HONOUR 1939-45: Leslie Allen, Arthur Bennett, John Cake, Stanley Cake, Ronald Cutler, Ernest Effemy, Hubert Harrison, Robert Johnston, Ralph Kemp-Welch, William Phillips.

It did not take long for Sopley to become saturated with sorrow in the months that followed August 4th 1914. The repetition of family names on the memorial is a poignant reminder that some families were very sorely afflicted. Two telegrams were received separately on the same day at Avon Farm telling of the deaths in action on the Somme of the brothers John and Gerald Bramble. The war was only a few weeks old when the Hon. John Manners lost his life at Villars Cotteret. It was in the previous year that his 21st birthday had been celebrated with a large estate party at Avon.

The wounds were many and deep and imperceptibly the old life was vanishing in the face of this impact. There is little specific village record of those years. Local people worked hard in support of the War Fund, the Sailors and Soldiers Wife Relief Fund and the Red Cross. A great Food Economy Campaign was launched in 1917 and there was full involvement in the Southampton County War Agriculture Society's scheme for the distribution of seed potatoes. A few miles away, at Heron Court and at Avon Tyrell, convalescent hospitals for wounded soldiers were established. Sopley's contribution to Gun Week in March 1918 was rewarded with the presentation of a 15 inch shell which was to be seen in the centre of the village until 1940. A dramatic reminder of a new dimension in hostilities was provided by an aeroplane accident at Sopley Park, also in March 1918. Physical horizons were widening rapidly, a development well illustrated by the following story of a Sopley parishioner, Sergeant B. He was in the No. 18 Machine Gun Squadron, attached to 22 Mounted Brigade, and was in Palestine in the Spring of 1918. While on duty, guarding a bridge over the River Jordan near Jericho, he noticed an Arab approaching from no-man's land, on the other side of which were the nearest enemy lines, not more than 800 yards distant. The Arab was mounted on a donkey, the only other noticeable feature being that the rider was perhaps smaller than the average Arab. Orders were that all who passed over the bridge were to be detained, so the Arab was kept prisoner for a day and a night until the guard was relieved. Sgt. B. who, as usual with our men, had learnt a little of the native language, spoke to the prisoner at intervals during the day, in Arabic. At 8 o'clock the following morning the sergeant returned to headquarters, taking his prisoner with him, a distance of about 4 kilometres. On handing over the prisoner to the Military Police, B. was astonished to hear the Arab ask, in perfect English, to be taken to the Brigadier, who was General Weigan. Subsequently Sergt. B. heard that the prisoner was no other than Colonel Lawrence (Lawrence of Arabia). The guard on the bridge on the following day reported that the Arab and his donkey returned across no-man's land the same way as he had come, probably penetrating through enemy lines, and by so doing joining the Arabs who were harassing the Turks on the other side.

POSTSCRIPT
(Reproduction of document 53M80/PZ5 from Sopley Parish Records, by kind permission of Hampshire Record Office).

In 1915 the National Registration Act ruled that all persons, male and female, born on 16 August 1850 or on any succeeding date up to and including 15 August 1900, should be registered. The enumerator for Sopley was C.F. Mason and those affected living in the village, at that time were:

SOPLEY STORES: Fred, Hilda, Henry & Mabel BERRYMAN.
                    Dorothy WRIGHT.
CHILTLEY HOUSE: Lydia & Lydia TREVOR. Mary COOPER.
SMITH'S ARMS: Albert & Bessie CUTLER. Lily SELLARS.
POST OFFICE: Mary, Walter & Arthur HARRISON.

107: The War to End All War

NEXT TO P O: John & Ellen BASTABLE; May PENNY & Ida CRABB.
PRIEST LANE: William & Hugh MILLS.
   George, Mary, Cecil & Eric HARRIS.
   George & Eliza BARROW; Harry STREET.
   George, Mary, Marjorie, Nora & Ronald FERGUSON.
PRIEST HOUSE: Charles, Emily & Chas. W. BUTTON.
RATFYN (Later MORDEN): Robert & Caroline MELSOME,
     Emily BROOMFIELD, Maud Penny.
WHEELWRIGHTS: Charles, Sarah, Helena & Eliza VINCENT.
MILL: George & Marth CRANTON; Rosa TUCK, George, Annie & Clara THORNER.
MILL COTTAGE: Leonard WATERMAN.
CHURCH LANE: John & Lily HARRISON.
PARK LODGE: Athelbert & Alice FREEMAN.
DAIRY HOUSE: Joe & Annie BENNETT; George STILLMAN.
HOMESREAD: Sarah FOYLE & Alice BURRY.
HOMESTEAD STABLES: Wilfred & Beatrice CUTLER;
     Agnes GIFFORD
SOPLEY PARK: John & Annette KEMP-WELCH, Warley & Annette PICKERING, Caroline SINGLETON, Martha WILLIAMS, Annie VEAL, Ida GREGORY, Nellie MARSH, Jane WHITWELL, William CUTHBERTSON.
WOOLPACK: Annie REEKS, Alice BRINSON, May CLARKE.
POLICE STATION: H.W. & Ethel ENGLEFIELD.
VICARAGE: Rev. & Louisa, Katherine & Nancy VALLINGS.
VILLAGE: Fred & Lily KIRLEY.
   Hester HARDY.
   George & Selina FREEMAN.
   Thomas, Sarah, Tom, Nellie, Daisy, Agnes & Frances DOWDING
   Charles & Sarah REEKS.
   Elizabeth, Alice & Violet HARRISON.
   Ed. Chas., Eliza & Charles BOYT.
   Joseph, Sophie & Elsie VIVIAN.
   Frank ELDON, Robert & Beatrice STRICKLY.
DERRITT LANE: James, Fred & Martha PENNY. William POPE.
   George & Jane WAYE.
   Geo. & Jane BARROW.
   George NICHOLSON & Albert KENDAL.
   William & Louisa WATSON.

Sopley Serves Again. 1939 – 1945.

Sopley's name was destined for widespread fame in World War 2, chiefly because of the activities in its midst of a branch of the service which was very much in its infancy in 1918. For thirty odd years from 1940 the name RAF Sopley was much talked about, first in awed whispers, then with growing confidence, and ultimately with pride and affection. Before further comments upon this story, reference can be made to a host of war-time activities, for which a variety of records is available, not least personal reminiscences.

The local Home Guard figures vividly among personal recollections. Its fixed headquarters was at the Assembly rooms and a mobile HQ was formed which functioned regularly close to river crossings, to Sopley Cross, and in the neighbourhood of RAF activity. Sgt. Farwell recalls the night when a vehicle ignored a request to stop at a mobile HQ close to the Avon Causeway. A bullet was promptly deposited in a rear tyre and after the vehicle slewed to a

Sopley Home Guard 1944
Back row (l to r): Jim Tuck, F. Penny, T. Moxham, F. Savoury, R. Childs.
Third row (l to r): H.N. Delia, B. Hodder, J. Hobert, R. Parker, H. Miles, M. Penny, Jack Tuck, H. Batt, A. Harrison.
Seated on chairs (l to r): B. Watson, A. Lambert, Cpl T. Russell, Sgt W.J. Farwell, Lt H. Kemp-Welch, Major R. Taylor, I. Fry, G. Nicholson, H. Stone, E. Fry.
Front row (l to r): F. Cake, W. Parker, W. Freeman, W. Mitchell, E. Carter, E. Effemy.
The trophy was for Lee Enfield 303 rifle shooting.
Photograph loaned by Phillis Bailey, Reg Harrison and William Farwell.

stop, it was discovered that the driver was the District Commanding Officer. He congratulated the sentries on their efficient attention to duty! The wives of the Home Guard members took turns in taking midnight hot drinks and sandwiches to the men on their lonely vigil and comment that present-day apprehensions about going out after dark never crossed their minds. The local sergeant's improvised intercommunication with his wife in time of emergency was the time-honoured police whistle. He recalls that while out shooting on Boxing Day 1940 he heard the urgent blast of his wife's whistle. The RAF were asking for provision of sentries that very night; patriotism and military discipline stood this test with difficulty.

It was quickly apparent that the war which some thought would be over by Christmas 1939 was going to last a considerably longer period, and for many months the emphasis was on a dogged survival. Sopley, together with hundreds of villages up and down the country, was caught in a busy whirl of ARP, First Aid, Salvage, Savings, Food Conservation and Food Cultivation. Allotment owners were urged to greater efforts, the collection of rose hips and waste paper suddenly assumed national importance. Some Sopley farmers and smallholders strove to enlist the support of the Acting County Surveyor towards suspending the one-way traffic system through the village on account of the time lost through adhering to it. In this they were unsuccessful legally, but they did receive the enigmatic encouragement that "other means would be found to give them the required facilities". Sopley's iron railings were listed in preparation for their removal to join the swelling tide of scrap metal for munitions. Together with Avon and Ripley, the village sacrificed its 15 inch brass shell from the First World War days to the same cause. Later in the year the Parish Council found itself making arrangements for the filling in of a bomb crater which appeared in the middle of the footpath leading from Ripley to Sopley through Mr Hibbs' field. A letter from the County Agricultural Committee encouraged people to keep pigs and form pig Clubs; attractive badges were later provided for this purpose, a white pig on a green background. In October 1940 the Red Cross Depot was moved from Sopley Park to the Homestead, and local farmers were urged to form a crop fire committee.

But it was the arrival of the RAF which caused the biggest local stir. Their caravans and bicycle parts could hardly have been a less pretentious overture to the ground radar operations in quiet country fields which led to the destruction of over sixty enemy aircraft by the end of the war. In the very early days the radar personnel were billeted locally until a proper camp was built nearby, the buildings of which remain to the present day. Among the first RAF personnel to arrive was Brindley Boon, later to become a Colonel in the

110: Sopley Serves Again

Sopley ARP & First Aiders. Second World War.
Mrs Hubert Kemp-Welch seated 3rd from left.
Photograph loaned by Phyllis Bailey.

Salvation Army. He recalls how he heard of his posting to Sopley early on Christmas morning 1940 and how he and a corporal travelled all day and at almost midnight

> *"drew up outside the massive iron gates of a location we were to come to know well as Sopley Park. Warned of our coming, the village policeman, Knight by name, with his bicycle, awaited our arrival and, as it was so late, decided to knock up the landlord of the local inn. In this way we spent our first night in Sopley at 'The Woolpack' – a new experience for me. The proprietor, Andrew Lane, was a bellringer, churchwarden and sacristan at the ancient church across the road and, with his wife, regaled us well into the next day with fascinating stories of village characters and their forebears.*

111: Sopley Serves Again

After a breakfast of ham, eggs, new bread, freshly farmed butter and a mug of steaming tea we expressed our thanks to 'mine host' and his gracious lady and made our way some 400 yards along the road to a permanent billet. We borrowed a wheelbarrow in which to convey our kitbags and other personal belongings.

Our new landlady was Annie Button. A charming lady in her mid-forties, she had arrived at Sopley some twenty years previously to teach in the village school. It was not long before she met Charles Button, a young farmer, and they were married. They ran the farm between them, Charlie spending much of his day delivering milk to the outlying areas and Annie feeding and watering the cattle and keeping a friendly eye on the poultry. Chickens had to be shooed off the kitchen table before we could sit down to meals.

Those first days of 1941 were particularly cold and there was a general shortage of fuel. The cottage completely lacked warmth when we arrived, and Mrs. B continually apologised for this and, as if to try to keep herself warm by auto-suggestion, went around the house singing "Some day my coal will come", set to a melody from 'Snow White and the Seven Dwarfs', then the rage.

Sopley was the first ground-controlled interception unit. Operations were carried out from a trailer in the middle of a requisitioned field. We soon became the eighth wonder of the world. Everyone who was anyone came down to be entertained by the fascinating new toy. Winston Churchill and Clement Attlee and other cabinet ministers; war lords; foreign diplomats; service chiefs; military brass hats – the lot. The crowning glory was the visit of King George VI. I was the fighter plotter that night. My job was to track the courses and calculate the airspeeds of friendly and hostile planes on a huge perspex grid reference map and to pass such information to the controller to be included in instructions transmitted to the pilot. The king was given a seat on my right, a curtain separating us.

We had been well briefed. Should the VIP speak to us we were to remember that he was there primarily as an RAF officer and we were to address him as 'Sir'. Never 'Your Majesty'! Imagine my state of panic when, right in the middle of a chase across the southern skies, the curtain was drawn aside and a deep, guttural voice asked: "And what are you doing?". I sprang to my feet and sent my chinagraph crayon hurtling to the floor, and replied in my best open-air voice, "Plotting, Your Majesty", as if I were about to plant a bomb under the throne."

112: Sopley Serves Again

> "Oh, are you", commented the king as he stooped down into the darkness to retrieve the crayon, which he calmly restored to a ledge on the plotting table. I deserved to be court-martialled for such an indiscretion. Instead, I was left with an illustration in humility that has remained with me for more than forty years".

(These extracts from an article in *The Musician* dated 7 August 1982 are reproduced with permission of Lieut-Col. Malcolm Bale, Salvation Army. Extracts loaned by Phyllis Bailey.)

And so war came to Sopley in a very intriguing form. The Smith's Arms became a Forces canteen, and the Woolpack a favourite retreat for service personnel. Romance dwelt in the quiet lanes and fields, and dances organised in aid of the Royal Air Force Benevolent Fund and other worthy war-time causes were well-attended.

Sorrow and bereavement were never very far away. The war casualty list did not reach the calamitous proportions of the First World War, but each sacrifice was no less real. Just as in the earlier conflict the eldest son of the Lord of the Manor of Avon was lost, so in 1943 the only son of the local 'squire', Sergeant Ralph Kemp-Welch, failed to return from a raid over Germany. Drama too stalked the neighbourhood. It was very shortly after the Commando raid on Bruneval that the local RAF commander solemnly advised local Home Guards to sleep with rifles very near to hand, as a reprisal raid on the local radar station was confidently expected at any time. Aircraft fell from the skies locally; Bransgore Churchyard contains the graves of eight allied airmen who were killed during the first half of 1943. A French fighter aircraft is reported buried in the swampy ground between the River Avon and St Catherine's Hill; the pilot's body was recovered.

Sopley has been described as the RAF station without an airfield. In April 1944 an airstrip was ready and the Americans started arriving in force; one crash-landed in Priest Lane. The road from Sopley to Bransgore (Derritt Lane) was, of necessity, closed to all road traffic, as both runways crossed it. Derritt Lane, before the construction of the airstrip, was much lower and subject in parts to considerable flooding, notably near Sopley Cross. It was built up with air-raid rubble brought from the stricken areas of Southampton and Portsmouth. A walk from Sopley to Bransgore today reveals the site very clearly; indeed 1988 pipe-laying operations in the same area must surely be presenting a strangely reminiscent picture to those who can remember the construction of the airstrip (sometimes taking the name of Winkton) nearly half a century ago.

113: Sopley Serves Again

It was a very busy village during the last twelve months or so of the war. The Forces Canteen was extremely well patronised, and the 'laundry on the hill' was in full swing, serving the needs of so many 'visitors'. In March 1944 the Parish Council resolved to call the attention of the District Surveyor to the dangerous condition of the Woolpack Bridge, owing to its having been severely damaged by army vehicles. Subsequent traffic developments have revealed that the long-suffering bridge is just as vulnerable in peace-time.

Soon the victory bells were sounding, application was being made to the Ringwood and Fordingbridge RDC for a grant of a shilling a head in respect of 130 children up to 14 years of age taking part in peace celebrations. The canteen was closed, Derritt Lane was re-opened, Home Guard and ARP uniforms were stored away, and the evacuees had all gone home.

Postscript

It is impossible to over-estimate the importance of RAF Sopley's contribution to the successful conclusion of the war. Through its fighter controllers and radar operators a really significant effect on the battle for control of the skies was achieved.

Following the end of the war, Sopley's role was confined for a short time to care and maintenance. But soon it was in full swing again, playing a vital part in a defensive radar chain. Excavations involved in these later developments ran into serious water-table problems. At one stage twenty-four pumps were working night and day, pumping water into Sopley Brook. Fears were expressed that the brook was being seriously contaminated because of this.

On 28 September 1974 trumpeters at RAF Sopley sounded the Last Post, the RAF Ensign was lowered, and a quiet leave was taken of the premises. Low cloud and driving rain prevented a symbolic fly-past by a Battle of Britain Spitfire and Concorde.

The camp was not destined to remain empty for long. There were rumours of a sports centre, an open prison, a holiday camp, and then in 1976 the camp was "captured" by the Household Cavalry for its annual training camp. The cavalry were welcomed in the locality on all sides, and their annual visits continued. For their part, the cavalry welcomed the training facilities available in the area, especially for cross-country work. Many of the horses seldom see grass during the very demanding life of ceremonial duty in London. The lighter and more entertaining horsemanship skills in their holiday camp training have included show-jumping, tent pegging, sword, lance, and revolver.

The sight of ceremonial Cavalry jingling through the roads of Sopley has enriched a tapestry already enlivened by elephants, tanks, juggernauts, and sheep. Possibly the most poignant and least predictable development was in 1980 when the following sign appeared at the gates of the old camp:

TRUNG TAM TIEP NHAN SOPLEY (Reception Camp, Sopley)

The camp had become a new homeland for the 'Boat people'. For a time there were members of 115 families living there, almost 600 people (including over 200 children) from many walks of life. It was possible to meet farmers, tailors, doctors, potters and boat builders and skilled people in a host of other trades. Most of them were Ethnic Chinese, who were resented by some Vietnamese. In just over twelve months Sopley had resettled more than a thousand people.

Reading Sopley Newsletters which were compiled at the time, and the records which were kept, it is clear that tremendous efforts were made by many people to alleviate the sufferings and anxieties which abounded. The depth of these anxieties is simply illustrated by the fact that when new arrivals at Sopley camp were invited to assemble on the enclosed tennis courts so that they could be organised, they were extremely reluctant to go in, fearing that this was to be their prison compound!

On a happier note, a group of children who were taken on a visit to the House of Commons in September 1980, were asked to write about their experiences. Extracts from these accounts include:

"In the House of Commons they lie down".

"In the House, no smoking, no camera and no steal".

"They are good men in the Commons".

This was another fight for freedom in an area where now the peace is disturbed only by plovers which in Springtime seek to defend their young by distracting walkers away from their nests with a mixture of aerobatics and menacing cries.

Sopley Miscellany

The majority of these extracts are taken from old editions of *The Christchurch Times* and are reproduced by kind permission of the manager of the Advertiser Series.

1856. April 12. For sale at 6s per hundred, 10,000 fir faggots lying in a plantation at Bransgore. G. Dewey, Bailiff, Harrow Farm, Bransgore.

1856. Sept 6. At a meeting in Christchurch to discuss the new railway, Captain Jackson argued that instead of a railway from Ringwood to Christchurch, it would be cheaper, more convenient, and in many respects to be preferred, if a horse tram-road was made, as they had in Paris and elsewhere.

1860. February. At the last cattle market in Ringwood, the supply offered for sale was as follows: Beasts 85, Sheep 467, Calves 28, Pigs 210. At the same market the quantities and average prices of corn were as follows:
   wheat 200 quarters, av. 43s . 6d. per qr.
   barley 234 quarters, av. 34s . 4d. per qr.

(1988. June. The last livestock sale at Ringwood Cattle Market took place on 29 June. Ringwood, a natural market centre for the products of farm and forest, received its Market Charter in 1226. Recent years have seen a steep decline in the numbers brought to the town for sale.)

1860. April. At a meeting of the Vales of Avon and Stour Farmers' Club, a resolution was passed that the cross with the Hampshire and South Down is the best description of sheep calculated for this district.

1860. Sept. Workman James Beazeley was buried and killed by a fall of gravel while working on the Ringwood-Christchurch Railway.

1862. Nov. 13. The Ringwood-Christchurch Railway opened. The line was used for 73 years and was finally closed on Sept. 30 1935. Before the arrival of this branch line people had to rely on carriers passing through the village. James Tilby's carrier left The Star at Ringwood every Tuesday and Saturday, for Christchurch via Sopley, and returned to Ringwood on Wednesdays and Saturdays. Charles Hodges' mail cart travelled from Christchurch to Ringwood daily.

116: Sopley Miscellany

1867. Sept. Mr Henry Whitcher's wheat rick burnt down through children playing with matches. Much property was miraculously preserved.

1893. Dec. 12. St Michael's Church, Sopley was severely damaged by storm. The nave roof was entirely stripped of its lead covering, and the lead in its descent injured the roofs of the Entrance porch and North Transept.

1901. Jan. New Year's Day. The New Year's Day sermon was preached by Rev. J.F.Vallings. At noon, aided by Churchwardens B.Goater and J.Bramble, the Tuck, Tulse, Tizard and Brown's Charities were distributed to the widows and deserving poor, and the Sopley Parish children attending school.

1901. June 9. Oddfellows of 'River Avon' Lodge, Sopley, paid their last respects to Brother Walter Tarrant of Ripley. No less than 30 officers joined in the procession wearing the regalia of the order under the leadership of Mr W.H.Butler, the Secretary. The cortege assembled at the crossroads, Derritt Lane, and marched through the village to the cemetery. On the conclusion of the service each Oddfellow repeated the word 'Amen' with hands clasped over the breast and dropped a sprig of thyme on the coffin.

1902. Jan. 18. In connection with Hampshire County Council Technical Education Scheme, Mr W.F.Gullick FRHS gave the first of a series of 4 lectures on the cultivation of flowers and fruit. There was a good audience at the Board School House.

1903. Serious diptheria epidemic in Sopley village.

1907. January. PC White (in Sopley for 7 years) moved to Damerham. PC Padwick moved from Damerham to Sopley.

1908. Mrs Edwards (neé Harrison) remembers seeing a convoy of four cars on their way from Highcliffe through Sopley to Heron Court. The German Kaiser was the VIP traveller.

1910. July 12. The Hon. Charles Stuart Rolls became Britain's first victim of powered flight when his French-built Wright machine crashed at a Bournemouth Aviation meeting. Mrs Hubert Kemp-Welch, living in Sopley in 1988, was a schoolgirl at that time at the school which later became St Mary Gate, Southbourne. She was in the sanatorium and through the window

117: Sopley Miscellany

witnessed the crash which took place on what is now a corner of St Peter's School playing fields.

1913. Sopley Mills Advertisement: Oat Flour 4½d per lb.
Oat Meal 4d per lb.
Rolled Oats 4d per lb.

1913. November. An unusual late Autumn event took place when some workmen repairing the roof at the Homestead at Sopley, disturbed a nest of wasps. The wasps swarmed round the workmen who beat a hasty retreat.

1926. August 21. Sopley Horticultural Society held its 20th annual exhibition in the grounds of Sopley Park. It was a huge success despite indifferent weather earlier on. Charles F. Mason was the Hon Secretary for the 20th time. Alderholt Prize Silver Band was in attendance, also Smith's roundabouts. Ladies of the Red Triangle Club produced a needlework display, F.G. Freeman sold honey, and H.R. Berryman again proved a capable caterer.

1937. December 11. Heaviest snowfall in Sopley for thirty years.

1938. February. Members of the Winchester and Portsmouth Diocesan Guild rang a peal of Grandsire Doubles on the bells of St Michael's, Sopley in 2hr 48min. The peal was of 5,040 changes, being 42 complete "six scores" in 12 different variations. Ringers: W.M. Stone, Treble; Edward T Griffin, 2; Francis W. Freeman, 3; Leonard G. Stone, 4; Francis G. Blake (conductor), Tenor.

1938. Nov 19. Mr William Caplin Morris, well-known Bournemouth builder and Church Warden at Sopley, met with a fatal road accident in Christchurch.

1942. February. The resignations of Rev H.E. Lewin from Burton, and Rev. D.F. Wright from Sopley, have left vacancies in two adjoining parishes and it has been decided that the two parishes shall be held in duality by one vicar. (Proposed as a war-time arrangement!).

1948. April. It was reported that the road had sunk at the main Sopley bus stop, causing a large pool of water in wet weather.

118: Sopley Miscellany

1952. September. Cats Eyes laid along the white line of the dangerous bend near Dismal Swamp, on the Avon Causeway.

1960. October. Battle of Britain Rememberance Service in Sopley Parish Church went very well until the organ was discovered to be smoking. It was disconnected and "Ye Holy Angels Bright" was sung unaccompanied.

1963. April. Bishop Cornwall blessed the new sixth bell in St Michael and All Angels Church.

Heavy Roller. Sopley Park, circa 1935.
Horses led by Tom Russell. Note the windmill in the background.
Photograph lent by Mary Russell.

Perambulation

A stroll through the village of Sopley of today, affords a rich experience of the readiness of Time to reveal its secrets to mortals who share its earthly stage for a while. Naturally perhaps, eyes are turned first towards the church, because it dominates, albeit largely unseen except from afar. The durability of the building is at once a tribute to the skills of our ancestors, and to the tenacity of the faithful who for more than seven hundred years, have planned and fought to preserve it for their successors. Standing as it does at the southern extremity of the village, with its commanding view of the Avon Valley to Christchurch and the sea, it is as though it has accepted, not only spiritual responsibilities, but the castle-like role of physical protector as well. In the mind's eye the tower becomes the keep, and under the wings of the iron-stone walls alongside it, village life has continued, unthreatened and free.

The mill below, at the water's edge, is the other centuries' old custodian of tradition in the village, but unlike the church, it became part of the prey of the

The Mill, Mill Cottage, and church tower.
Reproduced by permission of Basil White.

Priest House, Priest Lane.
(Bed and breakfast available).
Photograph lent by May Mould.

19th century invasion of Bransgore bricks. In 1878 it was extensively altered and enlarged, though its purpose remained unchanged until very recent times.

Alongside the mill, where a modern farmhouse now stands, is the site of the old manor farm house. Sopley Manor Court records are difficult and rare to find; but it seems likely that this old farm house was never the scene of court sessions nor the residence of the Lord of the Manor.

Time has scattered its clues all over the village, in the shape of thatch, other roofing, bricks, and filled-in windows. There seems little doubt that the fifty years following the advent of the Kemp-Welch family into Sopley in 1868, was a period of intensive brick-building activity. (The very extensive restoration of St Michael's Church which was carried out at that time was coincidental). The north and south lodges of the park, with their continental-style towers and turrets, were built in 1868. So was the building which was to become in turn the Smith's Arms and Fordwater Cottage. The Old Vicarage, Homestead (formerly The Elms and even earlier, Racedalls), and Sopley Park House were all added to or enlarged during this time. As the Victorian era drew to a close, and in the early years of the twentieth century, several dwelling houses which are still standing, appeared. These include the old Post Office at the entrance to Priest Lane, two or three houses on the now

The Woolpack, village homes, and the east end of the laundry.
Reproduced by permission of Basil White.

The Woolpack Inn, Sopley.
The name 'Louisa Reekes' is visible below the thatch line.
The laundry is visible to the left of the inn sign.
Photograph loaned by May Mould.

one-way stretch of road between the Woolpack and Chiltley House, Morden (formerly Ratfyn) on the high ground to the north of the church, and the laundry alongside Quamp, built about 1890 and displaying the first example in the village of imported, interlocking tiles. The stable building at Homestead appeared in 1910.

Many of the magnificent Sopley Farm complex of buildings, since converted very tastefully and imaginatively into private residences, also appeared during this hectic period of building. The old dairy house and yard, architectural gems in their own right, appeared in 1896, to be followed in 1910 by the great barn, probably the sturdiest building in the village, with its three feet thick walls which seem capable of withstanding all the tremors which modern road and air traffic can produce.

There are happily, domestic survivors from earlier times. Opposite the Vicarage, in Derritt Lane, stands the old granary which could date back to about 1650. An inspection of this fascinating building reveals that it was cleverly constructed so that it could be moved from place to place as convenience dictated. A hundred yards or so further up Derritt Lane, stands a venerable wattle and daub shed, the last relic of this method of building in the village. It used to be an appendage to a line of half a dozen old cottages close by which have been replaced by modern buildings.

It seems that the early years of the 18th century was another period of considerable building in Sopley. There was at least one brick kiln operating in the village in those days, and a good example of the earlier method of brickwall building can be seen in Priest Lane, in the house on the left hand side going towards Priest House. There the characteristic use of headers and stretchers may be observed in good measure, an attractive style of building which disappeared almost entirely with the advent of cavity walls. As has been noted elsewhere, Priest House was considerably damaged by fire in 1765 and it was several years before it was rebuilt.

'Smugglers', a prominent home in the centre of the village, and very recently rethatched, has been there since about 1720. Originally two houses or even three, it has been made into one, as have several buildings to the west of Sopley Brook. Smugglers is a compact lesson in domestic architecture, with its recesses, different levels, traces of baking ovens of long ago, and clever usage of beams.

The much-photographed and painted 'Woolpack', with its decorative thatch, has a schedule of deeds dating back to 1725. In that year, in a copy declaration of trust, (Footner to John Clapcott) it is referred to as the cottage. A release dated May 11, 1783 (John Clapcott to John Cook) seems to mark the start of its distinguished career as an inn.

123: Perambulation

Sopley Bridge and homes,
including the Apsidal North Lodge, entrance to Sopley Park.
Reproduced by permission of Basil White.

    A great number of the thatched roofs of the village disappeared with wattle and daub. Immediately to the west of the Woolpack bridge is a strongly built house where there are clear indications of the earlier existence of a thatched roof. The present roof is a pleasant mixture of old fish tiles and plain tiles.

    The camera bears witness to the comparatively recent departure of some thatched roofs and one or two complete cottages. One thatched cottage stood alongside the north lodge of Sopley Park; a beautiful flower garden now occupies its site. Another, in which village shoes were repaired for many years, finally disappeared with the straightening of the road towards Christchurch, alongside Sopley Park wall; apple trees grow in its place.

    Through the centre of the village runs Sopley brook. On its eastern 'shore' lie old piggeries and stables. Part of the western bank is occupied by colourful flower gardens. The remaining area, until the cultivated lawns of the Woolpack are reached, is a romantic mixture of brambles and deciduous trees. Here is the haunt of ducks and cats and occasional pasture for cows and horses. During the summer months the two halves of the village are effectively screened-one from the other. In winter a few lines of swaying communication are provided and the effect of this on a sunshine day is most agreeable.

The forge, another product of the late Victorian brick-rush in Sopley, together with the Smith's Arms and Sunnyside Cottage, form the gateway for the one-way system of traffic imposed just before the second world war. One of the many blacksmith activities which have faded from the scene, was the process of rimming wooden cart wheels with iron. The wheels would be made at the wheelwright's yard across the way; they would then be taken to the blacksmith where the heated rims would be fixed in place. Members of the younger generation would then be assigned the fascinating task of water-cooling the rims until the iron's embrace of the wheel was complete and almost indestructible.

Brick walls surrounding Sopley Park, Homestead, and Chiltley House, add to a lasting impression of a glowing red warmth permeating the old village. Even at the northern end, beyond the lines of modern houses, there is another multitude of bricks surrounding the cemetery with its attractive gateway – yet another late 19th century creation.

Sopley is not a place to wander in after dark. There is only one 'street light' in the village, fixed to the wall at the entrance to the assembly rooms. You will see little, and traffic may not see you. With this in mind it is safer to sit indoors and ponder the details that the daylight stroll has brought to light. How, in times gone by, the homes of the gentry and those of independent means were normally built facing south while the disposition of the workers' dwellings seemed much more haphazard, many facing east or west. And what was the origin of the beautifully hand wrought lightning conductors that now adorn the roof of a corrugated-iron shed in Derritt Lane?

"Homestead"
Formerly "The Elms", formerly "Racedalls".
Photographed by John Rowley-Morris from a painting loaned by the trustees of the Kemp-Welch estate.

The village green.
Sopley Brook and the ford may be seen, also Chiltley House to the right, Wheelwright's Cottage right of centre, and to the left, Quamp, and St Catherine's Hill beyond.
Photographed by John Rowley-Morris from a 19th century painting loaned by Bob Harrison.

"Smugglers"
In the heart of the village, with Sopley Farm buildings right and extreme left.
Photographed by John Rowley-Morris from a 19th century painting loaned by Bob Harrison.

In the heart of the village.
A 19th century painting looking from the Bransgore turning
to the Woolpack Bridge and Quamp.
Photographed by John Rowley-Morris, by kind permission of the Kemp-Welch estate.

Century of Memories

The physical world of Sopley has not been transformed since the turn of the last century. The blackcloths provided by St Catherine's and Ramsdown hills, Burley Beacon, and the distant tower of Christchurch Priory have scarcely changed at all and the River Avon continues its endless flow to the sea. Some village buildings have decayed, died, and been demolished; others have been adapted to changing needs. Here a great farm barn has been modified to become a splendid assembly room; there old farm buildings have had the modern architects' wand waved over them and have become residences for those whose work takes them away from home. But the church, the mill, and the "local" continue to cast shadows that have not really altered for far longer than one hundred years. Some cottages have lost their thatched roofs, some have not, but most would be readily recognisable still to those who joined in Victorian jubilee celebrations. The number of new houses in Sopley is quite small.

But if the setting is considerably unchanged, the details of daily life differ enough to reflect another ethos, perhaps another heart and soul. With the help of an oscillating time-machine, the habits and routines that are just within the living memories of a few can be recreated and stored.

In a farming community, machine-made noises were not far behind the crowing of the cock in the earliness of the hour. The centre of the village would frequently reverberate to the clanking of the chain and scoop device as the handle was turned and water was drawn from the brook and emptied into the horse-drawn water waggon standing between Fordwater Cottage and the old village Post Office at the entrance to Priest Lane. The village inhabitants often relied for their own drinking water on the spring at the northern of the two entrances to Sopley Park. Some yards further down the road, Sopley Farm Dairy would be busy pouring the day's milk yield into churns which would then be lifted on to the cart standing alongside and daily deliveries would commence.

Soon the unmistakeable noise of the solid-wheeled bus could be heard rattling its way along the road from Christchurch. Some servants of the community were to be observed in the course of their long and arduous duties with only their feet to carry them perhaps several miles a day. The carrier of letters was one, the forerunner — if that is the appropriate word here — of the postman, on his round from Winkton, through Sopley to Ripley, Shirley, and Avon. It is not so very long since, on Sundays and Holy Days, the Roman Catholic priest, the Rev. Mr Greening, walked from Christchurch in ill-fitting shoes to minister to his flock. His toe turned gangrenous and amputation did not stop mortification; he died and was buried at Sopley.

The Dairy House, Sopley Farm.
Photograph loaned by Montie Bates.

Throughout most of the nineteenth century there were two day-schools in the village, one next door to St Michael's Church and one a few yards up the road — which for long was called Avon Lane — from the present village store. This latter one was closed in 1895 when the school in Ripley was opened. From then onwards until the second world war there was a two-way traffic to learning. It was a familiar daily sight to see the Nonconformist children setting off along Priest Lane and thence via Church Way to Ripley. At some stage in their journey they would encounter the Church of England contingent making their way to Sopley. "Hello, Sopley bugs", "Hello, Ripley bugs", would sometimes be accompanied by the skirmishing between schoolchildren that is changeless. One pupil would ride his donkey to school all the way from Ripley, tethering it in the stables alongside the vicarage and walking up the hill to his place in the schoolroom beyond the church.

Just as Thursday is dustbin day in the village today, so in our Grandparents' time Monday was the day for two particular weekly routines. A disused laundry stands in the corner of the garden opposite the Woolpack car park. Thither very large wheel-barrows were trundled from Sopley Park House, full of laundry. Waiting for delivery in the steam-filled room would be several women. Water was pumped up to the laundry from the Woolpack stream to a tank in the laundry room. Inside was a formidable assembly of stove, copper,

The ploughman's homeward plod. Sopley style.
Harry Miles with Prince, Boxer and Cherry at Sopley Cross, circa 1935.
Photograph loaned by David Miles.

mangles, ironing tables, pressing tables, drying racks and flat irons of various sizes and weights. As labours progressed, so from the mill below the church a horse-drawn waggon, laden with flour, would be setting out on its weekly journey as far afield as Ripley, Avon, and Shirley, returning later in the day with a further consignment of corn. Apart from weighing facilities at the mill, there was a weighbridge close to the old Post Office, which was a favourite playground for the children of the time. Alongside, in the years between the two wars, stood a suitably mounted 15 inch shell. One of these was presented to each of Sopley, Avon and Ripley in 1919, marking the splendid contribution of the parish to Gun Week in March 1918. Doubtless when the folly of war engulfed the land again, the shells were sent to swell the response to War Weapons Week.

Every day the lovely smell of freshly-baked bread would permeate the air, from the direction of the village shop. The parish was still maintaining a considerable degree of self-sufficiency until very recent times. In 1878, in addition to those people engaged in the production of food, several and varied commercial activities are recorded. There were the wheelwright (Richard Corbin), the blacksmith (John Reeks), the shopkeeper (Maria Dowden), the carpenter, joiner and victualler (Joseph Tanner, Woolpack), dairy-man (Thomas Stainer), miller (G.O. Aldridge), postmaster (Charles Button), veterinary surgeon (Robert Blacklock), shoe-maker (Henry Butler). There

Sopley Stores in pre-war days.
Photograph loaned by May Mould.

were also four schoolteachers, one vicar (Rev. W. H. Lucas), one curate (Rev. E. J. Pope), and one Independent Minister (Rev. F. W. Turner). By 1915 the numbers are slightly reduced. Listed for Sopley are, the grocer (Henry R. Berryman), appartment hirer (Mrs Charles Button), blacksmith (C. Harrison), beer retailer (Albert Culter, Smith's Arms), victualler (Mrs Louisa Reeks, Woolpack), wheelwright (C. F. Vincent), subpostmistress (Mrs Mary Jane Harrison).

Self-sufficiency is also the keynote in the colourful story of entertainments for the village. Basic facilities were stronger in the summer than in the winter months, although the advent of the Assembly Rooms in 1934 went a considerable way towards achieving a stronger measure of seasonal balance. The Park was readily available for annual treats and flower-shows, for cricket and for bowls, and for the kind of Sunday-afternoon meanderings which so many English families enjoy. The field known as Quamp, which lies directly behind cottages 15, 16, 17 and 18 on the present one-way stretch of road, was for some years the scene of annual tug o' war competitions and less formal activities at varying times. The ground immediately due east of the Vicarage was the headquarters of the Sopley Association Football Eleven. The 'Woolpack', and for some years, 'The Smith's Arms', were focal points, not only for hard-earned refreshment, but also for any number of attendant activities. Until the arrival of the Assembly Rooms, the Church of England school on the hill was used for many social occasions. When the new school was founded at Ripley, the old British school, near the shop, ceased to exist, but its premises too were used for many years for concerts, social gatherings, Y.M.C.A., and the Red Triangle Club.

Some of the recollections just mentioned here will receive more detailed treatment in another chapter. For others, more of the colourful story follows immediately and what better starting point than the people themselves. The use of nicknames, particularily for inhabitants of the village, was very prevalent and compares vividly with the lack of them in our own days. The lads who swam the mill-stream, who boasted of salmon leaping into their arms, who tested to the full the durability of the village weighbridge, who sat on the Woolpack bridge and watched the elephants from a visiting circus ponder their way over the brook, all had their nick-names which soon completely eliminated any usage of those baptismal names given to them at the font. Teeler Harrison, Strip Harrison, Cronje Vincent, Tacker Butler, Doodle Eldon, Hobart Button, General Jordan, Nippy Cake. Was Cronje a Boer War label? Was Nippy a talented soccer forward? The answer to such questions must remain 'classified information' in history's solemn keep. "As the twig's bent, the tree's inclined." One mischievous pupil was soundly thrashed at school for poking a nettle through the gap in the dividing wall of the toilets and

"Sopley Jack".
Cup winner, Burley Show 1911, 1912, 1913.
Photograph lent by Bob Harrison.

stinging the anatomy of an unsuspecting teacher on the other side. This intrepid youngster grew up with a fascination for explosives. He led home-made firework expeditions after dark on the Quamp, with a mixture of gunpowder, sawdust and very short fuses. In the week following the birth of a young nephew in the village, he was at 'Teeler' Harrison's garage just across the road, fiddling with a gas cylinder. This was one which had come from the entrance to Sopley Park, where it was used to light the lamp at the southern entrance. The proud mother lying with her new baby was suddenly startled out of her wits by a loud explosion nearby. The gas cylinder had exploded with such force that parts of it landed in the Woolpack yard; the 'fiddler' was knocked out and whisky was rushed up from Woolpack to revive him. 'Teeler' seized the medicine and drank it with a transposition of the immortal words, 'Thy need is greater than mine'. Their boyhood behind them, they became absorbed in their specialised occupations in the community – the garage

The home of 'Tacker' Butler and 'Nippy' Cake.
Last traces of this cottage were removed during
post-war straightening of the Christchurch Road.
Photograph loaned by Leslie Freeman.

owner, the wheelwright and undertaker, the blacksmith, the mender of shoes.

And among them somewhere was he who chose his courting time with mature judgement, for the apple of his eye was a kitchen maid at the Vicarage and his weekly visit there was at eleven o'clock on a Sunday morning when the master and the mistress (Rev. and Mrs Vallings) were safely occupied with the faithful on St. Michael's mount!

Refreshment has been available in the strategic centre of Sopley, at the Woolpack, since well before the end of the eighteenth century. A schedule of title deeds relating to the property dates back to 1725, but between then and 1783 it is referred to simply as 'the cottage' and the traffic-battered bridge alongside bears the name of Cross House Bridge. It seems probable that the name 'Woolpack' is indeed associated with sheep farming; Vicar Willis was a pioneer in the popularising of Merino sheep breeding at the beginning of the 19th century. The proximity of the 'Lamb Inn' and Staple Cross is perhaps a further tangible reminder of the realities of considerable sheep farming activities in the Avon Valley.

On the Sopley corner which marks the beginning and the end of the one-way system of a later age, stands Fordwater cottage, built in 1868. This replaced an older dwelling which by 1898 for certain was known as 'The Smith's Arms', purchased in that year by Strong and Co. of Romsey. Unlike the landlords of the Woolpack, those of The Smith's Arms are listed as beer retailers only. In 1869 a law came into force requiring beer-houses to have a licence from J.P.'s, whereas previously only an excise licence was required. During the Second World War the Smith's Arms was a Forces canteen, serving the needs of the considerable numbers of armed forces in the immediate area. Since 1946 it has been a private residence, as 'Sunny Side' next door which earlier in the century was the site of 'Teeler' Harrison's workshop and garage. The petrol pump stood on the much-used parking space opposite cottages numbered 16 and 17.

Some of the names of those who hosted the inns in former times are given below. It will be seen that it was not uncommon to combine the duties of landlord with other work. Remembering the frequency with which customers must have arrived on horse back, it is not surprising to discover a combination of victualler and blacksmith:

WOOLPACK. 1859: William Shave (blacksmith); 1878: Joseph Tanner (carpenter, joiner); 1885: George Gilbert; 1890: Frederick Kerby; 1899: John Brinson; 1915: Louisa Reekes(Mrs).

SMITH'S ARMS. 1885: John Reekes (blacksmith); 1899: John Reekes; 1911: William Mills; 1915: Albert Cutler.

134: Century of Memories

The name of Mrs Anne Elizabeth Curtis is listed as beer retailer for 1939.

Inns in the parish were frequently used as the meeting place for societies and similar organisations. In 1903 a letter was sent from the Sopley section of the Oddfellows, with its headquarters at 'The Smith's Arms', to the Vicar, (Rev. Vallings), begging the use of the Church schoolrooms for further meetings of the Oddfellows, as the room allocated to them at 'The Smith's Arms' was no longer large enough to cope with the increased numbers.

It was not uncommon for inquests to be held at the Inns. On Saturday July 26th, 1856 an inquest was held at the Woolpack before Mr Pain, Coroner, and a respectable jury of whom W. Tice was foreman, on the body of Charles Stride, aged 14 years, who fell from a horse on the previous Saturday and immediately expired. It appeared from the evidence of witnesses that the lad was driving a waggon belonging to Mr. Whicher of Sopley, near the mill, where he was seen riding the leading horse and in a short time afterwards he was found by another man lying by the side of the road with his neck broken, and within a few yards of his father's house. A verdict of accidental death was recorded.

Sopley Garage in pre-war days.
'Teeler' Harrison's garage on the left (where 'Sunnyside' now stands).
Petrol pump in centre and old post office in right background.
Members of Freeman family in foreground, outside No. 17.
Photograph loaned by Leslie Freeman.

Sopley Smithy.
Early 20th century picture. Jack Harrison on left.
Photograph loaned by Charles Harrison.

In January 1907 an inquest was held at 'The Smith's Arms', Sopley, touching a newly born child. The jury, under the chairmanship of James Murray, returned a verdict that the child had been wilfully murdered by its mother.

A very unusual inquest, which came about as a result of a distressing accident, was held, not at one of the inns, but at Sopley House, in the park. In March 1918, an aeroplane piloted by Lieut. Claude Michael George Barrington, alighted in Sopley Park shortly before noon, the pilot having lost his way. A small crowd gathered round, and the pilot secured the services of some of the onlookers to hold the machine while he started the propellor. Unfortunately by some means, they failed to hold the machine and before the pilot could gain his seat it ran away uncontrolled. Miss Annie Veal was struck by the propellor and was killed instantly. Mr Fletcher of Winkton was run over but fortunately escaped unhurt, and another onlooker had a narrow escape, his pipe being knocked out of his mouth. The aeroplane eventually tripped up, and was brought to standstill by the propellor striking the ground. The police were summoned and removed the body of the unfortunate girl to Sopley House to await inquest.

Marquee.
A silent reminder of pre-war celebrations in Sopley Park.
Photograph loaned by Leslie Freeman.

In August 1913 the children of the Church School enjoyed their annual treat when they were taken for the day to Mudeford in six waggons, suitably bedecked, and kindly lent by local gentlemen. On the first day of this holiday month the children from Ripley Congregational Church Sunday School held their annual outing. Everyone assembled at the old British School at Sopley at twelve noon. The Rev. Mr Howarth asked for God's blessing on the day and all united in the singing of a hymn. A procession formed, headed by the Verwood Temperance Band. The procession wended its way to Sopley Park, where ample refreshment was available, and energy-consuming activities were soon in full swing.

Sopley Park was generously available for village annual red-letter days. One of these was the Sopley Horticultural Society show which, for example, in 1903, recorded upwards of six hundred exhibits, the prizes being distributed by Mrs Kemp-Welch and the sports prizes by Miss Beryl Kemp-Welch. Connolly and Bartlett's fun fair was usually in attendance. One year a drunken local inhabitant forgot to chain himself into the chair-plane attraction. He fell, heavily bruising himself, and the chair-plane ceased to spin from that day forward.

Sopley Oddfellows Centenary Fête, June 15th 1910.
Rev. James Vallings to right of choir.
Photograph lent by Doris Harrison.

At times of national rejoicing and on the occasions of annual treats and shows, Sopley was very much en fête. The lay-out of the village lent itself extremely well to processions and these were often a colourful and noisy part of the order of the day.

May 27th, 1903 saw the celebration of Empire Day and May Day for Sopley Church school. The day's proceedings began with a Church Service and this was followed by an assembly at the school where a talk was given on the British Empire. Then came a singing competition and festival at the old British School where the schools taking part were Sopley, Burton, and Thorney Hill. Everyone then repaired to the Vicarage grounds where tea, buns, races, and games were available. 'King Alfred burning the cakes' was performed and the press report of this includes the following comment: "and as it is supposed this great king burnt the cakes in this dear old parish, the play was all the more realistic!" To wind up the day's festivities there was the choice of the May Queen and dancing at the Maypole. An elderly lady, recently recalling the May-Day celebrations of 1910, observed:

> *"I have never forgiven Edward VII for dying when he did. That was the year I was going to be May Queen of Sopley and my one brief hour of glory was denied to me when all celebrations were cancelled because of the King's death."*

A partial calendar of activities for the previous year, 1902, bears adequate testimony to the vitality of social life in Sopley in those days. On 1st of May the traditional May Day celebrations were held, followed by dancing on the Vicarage field. On Monday, 30th June, a showery day, there were further celebrations to mark the coronation of King Edward VII. A procession of over two hundred children was marshalled at 1:30 p.m. and, enlivened with flags provided by the Committee, the procession marched from Priest Lane through the village to Sopley Park, to the inspiring music of the Verwood Brass Band. At 4 p.m. over 250 children were entertained at tea. The River Avon Lodge, the Sopley branch of the Oddfellows, held its annual fête, as did Ripley Congregational Church, on 2nd of August. Mr F.Freeman was the proud winner of the best-kept garden award on 16th August.

For a thinly-populated village, Sopley did well in competitive sport, fielding regular teams for cricket, association football, and (for a few years) bowls. During the years immediately before and after the turn of the nineteenth and twentieth centuries, the cricket weeks at Sopley Park were a feature of local sporting engagements. A keen cricketer, Mr J.Kemp-Welch used to invite famous players to take part in matches there. Among them was surely one of the brightest stars of the Golden Age of cricket, Prince Ranjitsinhji (better known as Ranji). He brought a team to oppose the local XI in 1900 and was himself dismissed for four runs.

The son and heir of the Lord of the Manor of Avon, the Hon. John Manners, was an outstanding sportsman. In 1910 he played a prominent part in the most famous of all the annual Eton v. Harrow matches at Lords, which Eton won when all seemed lost. The match is known to cricket lovers as 'Fowler's Match' but it might almost equally justifiably be called 'Manners Match'. He also played Lawn Tennis for Oxford against Cambridge. Barely three years after Manner's match, it is recorded that in mid-May of 1913 a Sopley cricket XI was well-beaten by a team from Lord Malmesbury's Heron Court. Playing for Heron Court was G.H.J.Bramble, one of the two brothers from Avon Farm who gave their lives on the Somme in July 1916.

Sopley Cricket Club records are very incomplete; but a record is existing of the annual meeting of the club on February 16th 1937. It lists Mr John Kemp-Welch as President; Major Eustace as Vice-President; Mr H.R. Berryman, Chairman; D.Boyt, Captain; L.Spiller, Vice-Captain. In 1936 the club played 21 matches, won thirteen of them and lost eight. Particular mention is made of the bowling of F.Pope, who took a hundred and one wickets at a cost of 4.2 per wicket.

Sopley Cricket, circa 1930.
Included are: **Back row:** 'Strip' Harrison (2nd from L), Charlie Button (3rd from L), 'Mudge' Watson (4th from L), 'Taffy' Harrison (5th from L).
Seated: Bill Freeman (1st L), Harry Stone (3rd from L).
Photograph lent by Reg Harrison.

Sopley Cricket.
5.20 PM. Who, when, where?
Photograph lent by May Mould.

Sopley Bowling Club was born when Mr Kemp-Welch made available a fine green, now built upon, in Sopley Park. Once again records are incomplete, but the following list of fixtures for 1938 reveals something of the club's scope and prowess:

May 26.	Sopley 61	Christchurch 45	Home	Won.
May 28.	Sopley 65	New Milton 52	Away	Won.
June 4.	Sopley 71	Gas Works 52	Home	Won.
June 11.	Sopley 59	Bmth. Co-op 65	Away	Lost.
June 15.	Sopley 53	Alexandra Park 53	Home	Tie.
June 25.	Sopley 60	Verwood 54	Away	Won.
July 9.	Sopley 54	Strouden Park 47	Home	Won.
July 14.	Sopley 55	Christchurch 61	Away	Lost.
July 16.	Sopley 62	Gasworks 55	Away	Won.
July 22.	Sopley 41	Ringwood 85	Away	Lost.

The successes and failures of the Sopley Soccer Club are more elusive. In the early days of the century the game was played in the field alongside the Old Vicarage, but in 1924 the club wrote a letter to Mr J. Kemp-Welch seeking a change of venue. The letter points out that the field is only just large enough, and that football there is sometimes a nuisance to neighbours. The letter goes on:

> "It has occurred to some of us that the Jocktrill Committee might be willing to allow football to be played at Jocktrill. There would be considerable advantage in having the upper end of the field levelled off, and now that the County Council have a road-widening scheme in hand in the Avon Road, it is thought that the Council would be willing to largely assist in this work for the privilege of having a convenient spot to dump spare soil."

Nothing materialised from this request, but not long afterwards the team was allowed to use a more suitable pitch in Sopley Park. A record exists of the annual meeting of the Sopley United Football Club under the chairmanship of Mr C.F. Mason, at the Red Triangle Club on 6 December 1926. After the conclusion of routine business the chairman eulogised the services rendered on the field by the captain, Mr Leonard Spiller. He had missed only one match in three years, and was presented with a table lamp on the occasion of his marriage.

141: Century of Memories

The variety and extent of religious, social, and sporting activity is readily discernible in the number of items reported in the local press of the time. It is possible to read of the Point-to-Point meeting at Neacroft in March 1913, of the many negotiations over the establishment of recreation areas at Shirley, Avon and Ripley, of Michaelmas Day celebrations, of the formation of a branch of the British Legion, of Scouts and Cubs, of the Sopley Brains Trust and the Ripley Band of Hope. Dances and concerts and magic lantern shows were held in the old British School until the Assembly Rooms became available. Picture a dark winter's evening, oil lamps burning, the combustion stove radiating heat at one end of the schoolroom. It was necessary to steer with great care and circumspection when guiding your dancing partner anywhere near the stove. Bodily contact with it could be uncomfortably warm. An improvised stage was available for the presentation of songs, recitations, and sketches, with the magic lantern in position, poised to provide lurid lighting effects. Musical accompaniment was unpretentious but effective. In a report on a concert in April 1867, at which £16 was raised for the church restoration fund, are the words:

> *"We believe that one opinion prevailed amongst the enthusiastic audience – that few villages in the south of England could have furnished such concord of sweet sounds as was heard on this occasion."*

The impact of world wars and the passage of another hundred years have combined to transport us many light years away from all this. There is a very unlikely story that in the 18th century there lived in the village a bad-tempered man named Seaforth who was known as the Sopley seer. He is reputed to have put curses on people to whom he took a dislike. He is also credited with having foretold the coming of the railways and the growth of a mighty town where Bournemouth now stands. Forgetting for a moment his reputation for evil ways, it is tempting to speculate what he might now forecast for this area for 2100 A.D...

Appendix 1

Land Tax Rate for the Tithing of Sopley – 1816.

Proprietor	Occupier	Rents £ s d	Sums assessed & exonerated £ s d	Sums assessed & not exonerated £ s d
Rev. J. Willis	for Vicarage	25 7 6		5 1 6
Rev. J. Willis	for Lanes	3 12 6		14 6
Rev. J. Willis	for Stradlings	9 1 3		1 16 6
Rev. J. Willis	for Groces	3 12 6		14 6
Rev. J. Willis	for Comptons	9 0¾		1 9 0¾
J. Elliott	J. Elliott	78 7 9¾	15 13 6½	
J. Elliott	J. Elliott	2 14 4½	10 10½	
Rev. Dr Windham	Tithes. J. Elliott	35 5 0		7 6 0
Stephen Marten	Tithes. J. Elliott	17 17 6		3 11 6
J. Elliott (late Poltney)	Tithes. J. Elliott	4 0 0		16 0
Wm Ward Wright	Wm Ward Wright	27 12 6		5 10 6
Richard Clapcott	Richard Clapcott	12 6 3		2 11 3
Bound (late Whites)	Robert Bound	15 13 6½		3 2 5½
Bound (mill)	Robert Bound	4 6 10½		1 5 4½
Bound (late Noris)	Robert Bound	12 10 9		2 11 8
Anne Gaffes	A. Gaffes	4 6 10½		1 5 4½
Thomas Woods	T. Woods	2 14 4½		10 10½
Edward Sabben	E. Sabben	12 18 9		2 11 8
John Spicer	Button	2 15 3¾	9 0¾	
Frances Oake	Thomas Blacklock	9 0¾		1 9¾
Ruth Elliott (Malt House)	John Elliott	2 13 9		10 9
James Tayler	J. Tayler	5 7½		1 1½
Edward Crouch	E. Crouch	1 8 9		5 9
Lady Fane	Stephen Groves	4 7	11	
Richard Wells	James Buckland	2 8½		6½
Wm White	Wm White	5 7½		1 1½
Moses Groves	Moses Groves	5 7½		1 1½
Wm Pollney	Wm Pollney	1 16 3		7 3

We the undersigned Commissioners do allow and confirm the within rate and we do appoint Robert Bound and Thomas Woods to be collectors of the same. Given under our hands and seals this 1st day of May 1816.

From the Red House Museum Archive in the Dorset Record Office. Ref D546/7064.

Appendix 2

Water

Although the village is flanked and bisected by a ready and natural supply of water in the shapes of the River Avon and Sopley Brook; and although the whole area abounds in springs and wells there were considerable problems before the advent of the mains water supply. Some of these problems were related to a superabundance of uncontrolled flow. At one time the Woolpack Inn and Bridge House opposite were inconvenienced by frequent flooding. Large areas of Jocktrill and adjacent land were more often than not under water; only an expensive and extensive operation of ditching and draining has improved this situation in recent times. Sopley Cross and surrounding lanes and fields were also subject to widespread flooding; here the creation of the war-time airstrip did much to reduce the flooding problem.

Squire John Kemp-Welch was for some time opposed to the establishment of a piped water supply for the village, because of his fear of contamination in an area where the height of the water table is often a potential problem.

Before the arrival of mains water supply at Sopley, two water rams were in use in the village. They were situated on the ground known as Butler's Moor, to the right of the road to Christchurch and south of the Woolpack and Bridge House. One pumped water to Sopley House and the other to the goldfish pond in the park. Everyone has heard of a water wheel and a windmill, both of which were doing duty locally, one at the mill, the other in Sopley Park. The water ram is not so well known and deserves more publicity, because of its simplicity and its durability.

It consisted of a pump of modest size of a type which was in widespread use during the 19th and early 20th centuries. Its function was to lift water to a tank or reservoir, often far above the level of the original water source. The local water rams used no fuel. They relied solely on the percussive power which the crystal clear water of two of Sopley's generous springs provided. Today, by peering through dilapidated and half-sunken "housing", it is possible to see still the two metal air vessels emerging from the gloom. Only the continued presence of a non-stop supply of life-giving spring water serves as a reminder of the erstwhile vital contribution of these now silent appliances. Together with the previously mentioned drinking water at the north entrance to the park, the vanished water-cart with its buckets and chains opposite the old post office, the pump at the laundry coaxing water from the brook at the Woolpack, and a large assortment of other wells and springs, they formed a picturesque "work force", more varied, if not so hygienic or scientific, as the pipes, taps, hydrants and clearing tanks of our own day.